Anglo-Saxon England Before the Norman Conquest: The History and Legacy of the Anglo-Saxons during the Early Middle Ages

By Charles River Editors

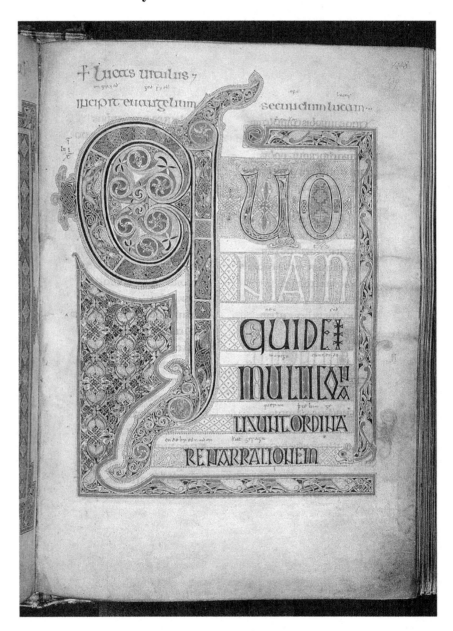

A medieval Anglo-Saxon manuscript

About Charles River Editors

Charles River Editors is a boutique digital publishing company, specializing in bringing history back to life with educational and engaging books on a wide range of topics. Keep up to date with our new and free offerings with this 5 second sign up on our weekly mailing list, and visit Our Kindle Author Page to see other recently published Kindle titles.

We make these books for you and always want to know our readers' opinions, so we encourage you to leave reviews and look forward to publishing new and exciting titles each week.

Introduction

A medieval English manuscript of the Gospel of Luke

The famous conqueror from the European continent came ashore with thousands of men, ready to set up a new kingdom in England. The Britons had resisted the amphibious invasion from the moment his forces landed, but he was able to push forward. In a large winter battle, the Britons' large army attacked the invaders but was eventually routed, and the conqueror was able to set up a new kingdom.

Over 1,100 years before William the Conqueror became the King of England after the Battle of Hastings, Julius Caesar came, saw, and conquered part of "Britannia," setting up a Roman province with a puppet king in 54 BCE. In the new province, the Romans eventually constructed a military outpost overlooking a bridge across the River Thames. The new outpost was named

Londinium, and it covered just over two dozen acres.

By the 2nd century CE, Londinium was a large Roman city, with tens of thousands of inhabitants using villas, palaces, a forum, temples, and baths. The Roman governor ruled from the city in a basilica that served as the seat of government. What was once a 30 acre outpost now spanned 300 acres and was home to nearly 15,000 people, including Roman soldiers, officials and foreign merchants. The Romans also built heavy defenses for the city, constructing several forts and the massive London Wall, parts of which are still scattered across the city today. Ancient Roman remains continue to dot London's landscape today, reminding everyone that almost a millennium before it became the home of royalty, London was already a center of power.

Shortly after Emperor Hadrian came to power in the early 2nd century CE, he decided to seal off Scotland from Roman Britain with an ambitious wall stretching from sea to sea. To accomplish this, the wall had to be built from the mouth of the River Tyne – where Newcastle stands today – 80 Roman miles (76 miles or 122 kilometers) west to Bowness-on-Solway. The sheer scale of Hadrian's Wall still impresses people today, but as the Western Roman Empire collapsed in the late 5th century, Hadrian's Wall was abandoned and Roman control of the area broke down.

Little is known of this period of British history, but soon the Anglo-Saxons – who had been harassing the Saxon Shore as pirates – showed up and began to settle the land, creating a patchwork of little kingdoms and starting a new era of British history. Several early medieval historians, writing well after the events, said the Anglo-Saxons were invited to Britain to defend the region from the northern tribes and ended up taking over. The Venerable Bede (672 or 673-735) said in his *Historia ecclesiastica gentis Anglorum* ("Ecclesiastical History of the English People") that in the year 449, "The British consulted what was to be done and where they should seek assistance to prevent or repel the cruel and frequent incursions of the northern nations. They all agreed with their king Vortigern to call over to their aid, from the parts beyond the sea, the Saxon nation. … The two first commanders are said to have been Hengist and Horsa."

However they came to control most of England, the Anglo-Saxons became the dominant power in the region for nearly 500 years, and the strength of their cultural influence could be felt even after William the Conqueror won the Battle of Hastings and became the first Norman ruler on the island. In the generations leading up to William's historic campaign, kingdoms fall, others rose, and the kingdom of England took shape under the guiding hand of kings like Alfred the Great and Æthelstan. This period of history was undoubtedly the most famous in Anglo-Saxon England, with countless video games, novels, and shows depicting the Great Heathen Army's invasion of England in the 860s and King Alfred's reign in the face of their incursion. At the same time, the Anglo-Saxons forged enough of a national culture that when William did conquer the island, the efforts to consolidate his rule in England were complicated from the start, both due to external enemies and those jockeying for his position while he was still alive. The Normans would manage just barely to cling to power over England, and William remains the last foreign conqueror of the island.

Anglo-Saxon England Before the Norman Conquest: The History and Legacy of the Anglo-Saxons during the Early Middle Ages looks at how the Anglo-Saxons and England managed the turbulent centuries before William the Conqueror, particularly the beginning of the Viking raids. Along with pictures depicting important people, places, and events, you will learn about the Anglo-Saxons like never before.

Anglo-Saxon England Before the Norman Conquest: The History and Legacy of the Anglo-Saxons during the Early Middle Ages

The Rise of the Anglo-Saxons in England

At the time of Julius Caesar's first visit to Britain in 55 BCE, Romans knew very little of this mysterious land, and myths and legends about the fearsome Druids and blue-painted savages abounded in the Roman world. By the late 1st century CE, Britain was securely established within the Roman Empire and becoming an increasingly important and wealthy province that ultimately produced Roman Emperors of its own. The transition from a wild misty backwater into this wealthy addition to the Empire was not without difficulty. Rebellions, particularly those staged by the Iceni, were frequent occurrences. The savagery of these rebellions was such that it is difficult to understand how Roman rule was not only preserved, but how the process of Romanization, proven more successful in Britain than in most non-Latin provinces of the Empire, was achieved.

The reasons behind this success lie in the nature of the island's political situation, which facilitated a Roman policy of divide and rule. This was used in successful combination with their normal carrot and stick approach to pacifying what, for all intents and purposes, should have been an impossible challenge, seeing as how the Romans were operating so far from their center of power. The Britain invaded by Caesar in 55 BCE was populated by a large number of Iron Age tribes, all of which belonged to a broadly Celtic culture. In the context of Britain, however, the term "Celtic" must be seen as a linguistic one, because despite suggestions of deep-seated cultural links with the Celts of Northern Gaul, there is, in fact, very little evidence of permanent, strong ties between the Celts in Britain and those in Gaul.

Andreas Wahra's picture of an ancient bust of Caesar

Caesar's expeditions to Britain in both 55 BCE and 54 BCE have to be viewed against the backdrop of the political situation in Rome at that time. Caesar had control of a large army in Gaul, and his campaign was, to a very large extent, undertaken on the pretext of combating an external threat to the empire. This justified the maintenance of his control over these forces at a time when there was a move in Rome for him to be relieved of his command even before the end of his commission, which was scheduled for 54 BCE.

Thus, Caesar was determined to retain command of his troops at all costs, which was pivotal to his political plans. As outlined in his *Gallic Wars*, he claimed the Britons had been aiding the Gauls and posing a very real threat to the Roman attempt to pacify the newly-conquered country.[1]

The English Channel was generally regarded by the Romans as defining the very edge of the world, and the symbolic significance of crossing the "Ocean" was not lost on Caesar, intent as he was on projecting himself as Rome's greatest general and politician.

Whatever the original aim, it is clear the Romans had initially intended to land at Dover, but upon arrival offshore, the numbers of assembled tribesmen on the cliffs persuaded Caesar that discretion was the better part of valour, and he sailed a further seven miles up the coast to what he thought was an unguarded beach—now thought to be Pegwell Bay on the Island of Thanet—and landed there.[2] The establishment of a beachhead proved extremely difficult, as the British fiercely opposed the landings and were only driven back by ballistae fired from ships anchored off the coast.

A camp was established. Caesar received hostages from the surrounding tribes, but he was unable to consolidate his bridgehead as his cavalry did not arrive. He quickly realized he had not come equipped to deal with a typical (harsh) British winter. Aware of his precarious position, Caesar decided to return to Gaul rather than risk being stranded in Britain over the winter with the very real possibility of complete defeat. He successfully crossed back to Gaul and continued to receive hostages from two tribes on the southeast of the island. The other tribes, however, believed the threat from Rome to be over and decided not to honor their pledges.

No matter how this particular campaign is assessed—either as an intended invasion or a reconnaissance mission—it failed to achieve any real goals. Despite this, the Senate, awed by the fact that Caesar had gone beyond what they regarded as the "known world", declared a supplication—or thanksgiving—of 20 days in honor of his achievements.

On his return to Gaul, Caesar immediately began to plan for a second invasion, scheduled for 54 BCE. Cicero referred to these plans in letters to a friend, asking him to make sure he acquired a British war chariot for him.[3] The Romans had learned from their mistakes in 55 BCE, and instead of invading with only two Legions, on this occasion, the force was comprised of five plus 2,000 cavalry, and all personnel were carried on ships specially designed for beach landings. He also planned his supply route more carefully and leaving Labienus at Portus Itius to oversee the regular transport of all food and other equipment necessary to maintain an invading force.

The Romans landed at the spot Caesar had identified the previous year, but this time their landing was unopposed. As soon as the bridgehead was established, Caesar ordered Quintus Atrius to advance inland. By the end of the day, this force had covered nearly 12 miles and defeated a British force at Bigbury Wood.[4] The next day, the Romans prepared to march further

---

[1] Julius Caesar, *Commentaries on the Gallic Wars*, 4.20. (Trans. by W. A. McDevitte and W. S. Bohn) [Online]. Available at: http://www.forumromanum.org/literature/caesar/gallic_e1.html

[2] Julius Caesar, *Commentaries on the Gallic Wars*, 4.25. (Trans. by W. A. McDevitte and W. S. Bohn) [Online]. Available at: http://www.forumromanum.org/literature/caesar/gallic_e1.html

[3] Cicero, *Letters to Friends*, 7.6 and 7.7.

inland, but a severe storm that wrecked numerous invasion fleet vessels caused Caesar to order his troops back to the coast for repairs.

In early September, Caesar marched inland once again, confronting the forces of Cassivellaunus, the king of a tribe living north of the Thames. Cassivellaunus had recently successfully defeated the Trinovantes and was now their war leader, as well. With a combined force, the Britons harried the Romans but realized they were not strong enough to inflict a decisive defeat on the invaders. Caesar continued his progress northwards, but the constant attacks meant that by the time he had reached the Thames, that one, fordable crossing had been heavily fortified by the Romans who had used an elephant to terrify the Britons and the defenders into abandoning the crossing due to fright.[5] The Trinovantes sent ambassadors promising aid and provisions against Cassivellaunus and the Romans restored Mandubraccius to the Trinovantine throne. Other tribes followed the Trinovantine lead—including the Cenimagni, the Segontiaci, the Ancalites, the Bibroci, and the Cassi—and surrendered. Caesar, now in a more secure position, laid siege to Cassivellaunus' last stronghold at Wheathampstead.[6]

As in the previous year, Caesar was eager for a resolution to the conflict and was fearful that he would be stranded in Britain over the winter. Consequently, he did not press the siege, and when Cassivellaunus offered to provide tribute and hostages and agree not to attack the Romans' new allies, the Romans agreed to the terms and promptly left the island. No garrison of any sort was left in Britain to enforce the settlement, and it is not known if any tribute was ever paid.[7]

Britain did not officially fall under Roman rule until 43 CE under the reign of Emperor Claudius. It should, however, be clarified that the entire island was never fully under Rome's control, and even what Rome was able to conquer was the product of the labor of several generations. This led to a periodic shifting of the borders along Rome's frontier, solidified in the construction of Hadrian's Wall (122-138 CE) and the later Antonine Wall (141-158 CE). The latter wall, probably a structural "advance upon Hadrian's turf wall" (Hornblower, Spawforth, and Eidinow), was merely a brief attempt to advance Rome's borders farther into modern-day Scotland. However, archaeological surveys suggest a "single period of occupation" from ca. 139-158 CE, and the wall was gradually abandoned and demolished around 163 CE (Hornblower, Spawforth, and Eidinow). Afterward, Hadrian's Wall was reoccupied, and the border between the northerly Picts of modern Scotland and the Romans was redrawn. The territory comprising modern-day Scotland was never "conquered and incorporated into the Roman Empire" (Higham and Ryan 21). Rome's iterative conquest of much of Britain did eventually begin to bear fruit, to the effect of historian Tacitus calling the island rich. The reality was, however, that Rome's occupation was "probably a drain on imperial resources for a century and more" (Higham and

---

[4] P. 22, *Britannia: History of Roman Britain* by S. Frere (1987). Routledge: London.
[5] Polyaenus, *Strategems*, 8.23.5.
[6] P. 25, *Britannia: History of Roman Britain* by S. Frere (1987). Routledge: London.
[7] Caesar, *Letters to Atticus*, 5.

Ryan 21). Even though it yielded "highly valued" products such as pearls, hounds, and tin, the island was "economically marginal" and cost more to retain than what could be plundered (Higham and Ryan 22).

An ancient bust of Hadrian

A section of Hadrian's Wall

Rome's presence in Britain was what Higham and Ryan call a "frontier society" (22-23). This was characterized by the distribution of local garrisons across the landscape, the largest being in Caerleon, Chester, and York. This settled garrison's, *vici* in Latin (from which the suffix -wick and -wich in place names such as Warwick and Norwich derive), were effectively "small islands of governmental influence within the wider landscape" of Britain (Higham and Ryan 24). The caliber of Roman urban colonization characteristic of *colonia* (colonies) such as Londinium (London) was a minority. These "islands" would have been an interesting mix of ethnic and religious identities, as the legions drew from all over the empire (Higham and Ryan 25) and exhibited a form and style of development similar to that of towns in the American West in the

19th century, as businesses and other semi-urban outcroppings grew out of these little centers of Roman rule (Higham and Ryan 23-24). These Roman settlements marked a point of demarcation between Roman Britain and "Celtic" Britain, as "the indigenous population lived in enclosed settlements that changed little in consequence of Roman occupation beyond the appearance of a few pots, small items of metalwork and cheap jewelry" (Higham and Ryan 24). There is a seeming lack of extensive integration and development of Briton characteristics in other provinces, such as Gaul.

Late Rome's instability did not just affect the empire and its territories but also its neighboring peoples and nations. The Western Roman Empire's bureaucratic breakdown in the provinces of Gaul and Britain "affected [Germanic] communities beyond the Rhine," as young men took to raiding the now vulnerable Roman lands in southeastern Britain and northern Gaul (Higham and Ryan 34). One such Germanic group was the Saxons. The earliest mention of their activity in Britain was their raids in 364, documented by Ammianus Marcellinus (Moreland). Another early mention of the Saxons is the so-called "Barbarian Conspiracy" of 367 when Britain was attacked by Saxons, Picts, and Scots. The exact scale of these incursions is uncertain, since Ammianus Marcellinus is once again the only source for the event, and it is "unclear how significant these events were," since the report "was highly political," and therefore, probably exaggerated (Higham and Ryan 34). Archaeological evidence of Roman forts and other sites occupied in the 4th century suggests that Britain and northern Gaul were targets of North Sea raiders (Higham and Ryan 34). Likewise, Ammianus Marcellus attested to supposed Saxon activity in northern Gaul in 367 (Moreland).

Saxons were more likely actively raiding southeastern Britain by as early as the 3rd century. The Saxon Shore (*Litus Saxonicum*) was the name given to the coasts of southern Britain, guarded by an affiliated series of 10-12 forts constructed from the 3rd century to about 330, and they were commanded by the count of the Saxon Shore (*Comes Litoris Saxonici*) (Moreland). How this shore came to be named for the Saxon is a matter of some debate. Two arguments are that the shore is so named for the Saxons who either manned the forts as employed Roman mercenaries or harassed the shore and gave their name to the forts constructed to oppose them (Moreland). The shore, its forts, and associated command were ultimately evacuated by Emperor Constantine III in the early 5th century, leaving it open to attack (Moreland 41).

It is difficult to determine exactly when North Sea Germanic people began settling in Britain since the argument is constantly being refined by further scholarship and archaeological inquiry, but the traditional stance is that it began around the early 5th century. The 5th century in Britain was characterized by a decline in Roman urbanism and a transition to new styles of architecture and settlement. Nicholas J. Higham summed it up by noting, "Certainly, at settlement after settlement, it becomes increasingly difficult to find evidence of Roman-style activity. Numerous sites reveal what has been termed "squatter" occupation[s], denoting the end of a Romanised [sic] lifestyle, with elite residences no longer maintained and/or converted to agricultural functions, then abandoned altogether. Occupation of many towns seems to have shrunk across the late fourth century to the point where large parts of the walled area were unoccupied."

This early 5th-century influx of Anglo-Saxon migration is characteristic of the broader phases of the migration period, called *Les Invasions barbares* (the Barbarian Invasions) in French or the *völkerwanderungen* (the wanderings of peoples) in German. The Anglo-Saxon settlement of Britain was a smaller part of a larger historical era in which Europe Germanic, Slavic, Arab, Celtic, and various Eurasian people were on the move, often resettling in Roman lands (Halsall 35-55). These migrations happened in two large waves, first in the 370s and then in the 410s (Higham and Ryan 34), and archaeological traces of North Sea Germanic activity in sub-Roman Britain suggest the Anglo-Saxons began seriously settling in Britain during the second wave. The specific archaeological finds with evidence of the Anglo-Saxons' presence include styles of burial and associated grave finds, such as brooches and swords. An important caveat is that it is a pitfall to associate a specific style of artistry—such as here, in metalwork grave finds—with a single ethnic group as specific styles and patterns do not necessarily belong to a single or certain ethnic group. Further, if said style carries enough prestige, it will be emulated by other cultures and peoples (Ian Wood 429). The evidence is not only archaeological but also literary, and this is where the discussion of Anglo-Saxon settlements becomes quite nebulous, and special care should be taken with the sources.

Perhaps the most influential primary source on early Anglo-Saxon history in the Venerable Bede (c. 673-753), a Northumbrian monk most famous for his *Ecclesiastical History of the English People* (c. 731). This history is a paramount source for the 7th and 8th centuries of Anglo-Saxon history, but Bede also had a fascination with what he called the "*Adventus Saxonum*" (the "Arrival of the Saxons"), which he took to be "foundational to English history" (Higham and Ryan 72). For this reason, he began his narrative of the Anglo-Saxons, his people, with their origins.

It is important to understand what Anglo-Saxon means and to whom it refers. Those who are today called the "Anglo-Saxons" were rather loosely related and independent North Sea Germanic people. They were comprised of Saxons from northwestern Germany, Angles from southern Denmark (Davis), and the often-forgotten Jutes from the Jutland peninsula in Denmark (Higham and Ryan 74). It is thanks to Bede that modern societies call them Anglo-Saxons, as he wrote of their coming to Britain in his "Greater Chronicle" (c. 725): "The people of the Angles and the Saxons were conveyed to Britain in three long-ships. Bede followed the typical 8th-century convention in referring to *all* Anglo-Saxons as *Angli* (Angles or English), which is why it is the *Ecclesiastical History of the English People*. By the 8th century, the Anglo-Saxon nobility "no longer distinguished themselves (if they ever had) on the basis of ethnic and political identities determined on the continent" that is mainland Europe (Thacker 469). Further, Bede was not the first to refer to the Anglo-Saxons under the collective term of *Angli* (Thacker 470). While "Saxon" seemed to have been the dominant self-identifying term among the Anglo-Saxons for a time (many Angles, such as the Northumbrians, labeled themselves Saxons for a time) since "Roman times," the term, "English," won out (Thacker 469). Therefore, while Bede's work refers to the Adventus Saxonum, the "Arrival of the Saxons," when narrating the arrival of the Anglo-Saxons in general, he *chose* to align himself with the current trend of defaulting to calling them all "English" (Thacker 469).

While Bede is certainly one of the most influential sources, he is not the only one—and by far not the closest—to the period of Anglo-Saxon settlement. The early 5th century in Britain is surprisingly well-documented up to 410, when there is a sudden cut off in primary sources (Thacker 469). Further, there are a specific host of resources that Bede seems to have relied upon for this period and incorporated into his narratives: Gildas's *De Excidio et Conquestu Britanniae* (On the Ruin of Britain) (mid- to late 6th cent.), Constantius of Lyon's *Life of St. Germanus* (c. 460-480), St. Patrick's *Confession* and *Epistle* (mid-5th century), a letter from Gallic Bishop Sidonius Apollinaris to a supposed Namatius (c. 480), which refers to Saxon pirates, and *the Gallic Chronicle of 452* (Higham 73-76). That is a lot to unpack, but there is more. Christopher A. Snyder, in his work, *An Age of Tyrants* (1998), takes the perspective of the Britons in this time period and compiles a list of primary sources, including many of the ones just mentioned. He mentions a few others that add to an already long yet still too short list of primary sources: the aforementioned Ammianus Marcellinus's multiple volume history, titled *Res Gestae* (c.390/91), the aforementioned *Notitia Dignitatum* (5th century) which details specific 4th- and 5th-century Roman offices in Britain, and several later sources, such as the *Anglo-Saxon Chronicle* and the *Historia Brittonum* (*History of the Britons*), written by the Welsh monk Nennius (Snyder 30-46). Many of these primary sources, excluding Bede, are quite short and can be found online. They offer a firsthand glimpse into the period of late Roman Britain and Anglo-Saxon settlement, as seen by thinkers temporally near to the events. Further, the value of such an exercise is that it encourages the reader to come to his own conclusions and draw his own picture of the period. Another bonus is that it will make the reader less reliant on historians as secondary sources such as this one and puts the reader on level intellectual ground when reading them.

The question remains what to make of these sources and how Bede draws on and interweaves them in his narrative. In other words, what do people know happened during the Anglo-Saxons' settlement of Britain from these sources? The traditional narrative of the advent of the Anglo-Saxons is that sometime in the early 5th century, they sailed from their homes in northern Germany and southern Scandinavia to serve as mercenaries for the already declining Romans, fighting against the invading Irish to the west and the Picts to the north. After establishing settlements of their own, they eventually turned on their Romano-British patrons and claimed much of Britain for themselves. This narrative is due almost entirely to Gildas, thanks to Bede's reliance upon it.

Gildas took a British perspective in his *De Excidio et Conquestu Britanniae*, and his monograph is not a historical work *per se* as it would be understood today; it had a clear thesis and was concerned with an overarching theme instead of chronicling specific events (Higham and Ryan 51). The crux of Gildas's monograph was that the Britons were "a new chosen people, a 'latter-day Israel' as he put it," who had become sinful and had lost their way (Higham and Ryan 57). Therefore, the Saxons, as he saw it, were God's divine punishment on a fallen people, relying heavily on Old Testament themes and imagery. It is also from Gildas that a part of the myth of King Arthur grew, as he accounts for a moment of Briton victory over the invading

Saxons under the leadership of a certain Ambrosius Aurelianus at Badon Hill. This Roman military leader is claimed by some to be the "historical Arthur." As a work of history, Gildas consistently botched his dates and chronology, especially in comparison to other sources (Higham and Ryan 57-65). Regardless of the text's historical merit or lack thereof, the Saxons' narrative of being invited by the Romano-British to help them in their wars against the encroaching Irish and Picts is the dominant one, present also in Bede. Gildas created the character of Vortigern, a British tyrant or ruler who invited the Saxons, led by semi-mythical brothers Hengest and Horsa, who later turned on the Britons to establish a proto-English nation. Bede drew heavily on this in his account of the coming of the advent of the Anglo-Saxons.

So, to summarize the material, the early 5th century witnessed a decline in Roman urbanism and settlements and an increase in the presence of burial patterns and grave finds characteristic of North Sea Germanic people. Likewise, primary sources such as Gildas and *the Gallic Chronicle 452* attest that the Anglo-Saxons staged a violent takeover of Britain by the mid-5th century, though the archaeological evidence suggests they were present earlier than that. Further, as will be seen in the examination of the earliest Anglo-Saxon polities and societies, the narrative of the violent conquest of Britain, the triumph of one peoples over another, is more a construction of the primary sources. History is much more complicated than that. Whatever the truth of the matter, by the 5th century CE, the Anglo-Saxons were there to stay.

Early Anglo-Saxon England

The Venerable Bede, in chapter 15 of his *Ecclesiastical History of the English People* (c. 731), had this to say about the early Anglo-Saxons: "They came from three very powerful German peoples, the *Saxons*, *Angles* and *Jutes*. The people of *Kent* and the inhabitants of the *Isle of Wight* are of Jutish stock and also those opposite the Isle of Wight, that part of the kingdom of the *West Saxons* which is today still called the nation of the Jutes. From the land of the Saxons, that is the region now called the land of the Old Saxons, come the *East Saxons*, the *South Saxons* [and] the *West Saxons*. And besides, from the land of the *Angles*, that is that homeland which is called *Angulus*, between the provinces of the Jutes and the Saxons, which remains deserted from that time right up to the present, came the *East Angles*, *Middle Angles*, *Mercians* and the whole race of the *Northumbrians*…Their first leaders are said to have been two brothers Hengest and Horsa, and later Horsa was killed in battle by the Britons and in the eastern part of Kent there is a monument bearing his name. They were the sons of Wihtgisl, whose father was Witta, whose father was Wecta, whose father was Woden, from whose stock the royal families of many kingdoms claimed descent. (Higham and Ryan 72-74)[8]

---

[8] Italics my own.

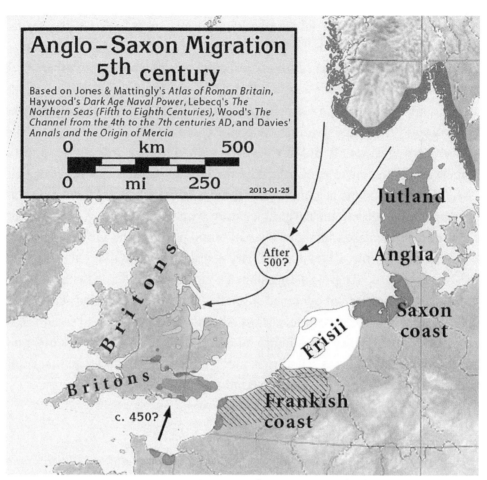

A map of the migrations in the 5ᵗʰ century according to Bede

This account gives the standard geopolitical spread of the Anglo-Saxon England that many may conjure in their minds when considering the period. It is the famous heptarchy, the division of Anglo-Saxon England into seven kingdoms: Northumbria, Mercia, East Anglia, Essex (East Saxons), Sussex (South Saxons), Wessex (West Saxons), and Kent. Astute readers will realize that this division cuts out the Middle Angles and the Jutes of the Isle of Wight. As an aside, Higham and Ryan have proposed that the migratory patterns of the Angles, Saxons, and Jutes were determined by Britain's rivers and bodies of water, with the Saxons and Jutes settling along the Thames and the English Channel and the Angles along the Humber and other rivers in northwestern Britain (107). The issue with Bede's account is that it was a late addition, probably conceived while in Canterbury, and has more to do with the geopolitics of the 8ᵗʰ century when he was writing in the late 4ᵗʰ and 5ᵗʰ centuries, when the earliest Anglo-Saxon polities and kingdoms began to rise (Higham and Ryan 75). Further, Bede's account is mirrored quite closely in the version found in *The Anglo-Saxon Chronicle*, which uses much of the same language ("The Anglo-Saxon Chronicle"). What is important to take away from Bede is his pervasive division of the Anglo-Saxons into three "tribes" or "peoples"—the Angles, Saxons, and Jutes— and that he associated them with specific places and later 8ᵗʰ-century kingdoms.

Fledgling Anglo-Saxon kingdoms arose in south and southeast Britain in the 6ᵗʰ century. Helena Hamerow sums up the kingdom-formation quite nicely: "Instead, the transformation from

Roman Britain to Anglo-Saxon England was seen as having been carried out by a tiny, military elite aided by the processes of exogamy, assimilation and exchange." (Hamerow 268)

These polities were not the continental aristocratic kingdoms with definite borders one might want them to be. The early kingdoms were established in a world belonging to landowning farmers rather than the king. Archaeological studies at cemeteries and settlements indicate a society that "was not rigidly stratified" (Hamerow 276): Hamerow explained, "Access to power and wealth was not primarily determined by birth, and rank was dependent in large part upon factors such as age, gender, descent and the ability to amass portable wealth, although control over land presumably also played a role." (Hamerow 176).

The argument can be made that early Anglo-Saxon society was much more egalitarian, and the emergence of high-ranking dynasties was something learned from the culturally prestigious Franks. This will be dwelled upon more later. Early Anglo-Saxon society prioritized kinship (*cyn* in Old English) and was the basis for tribal relations, organized around the farming landholder, (O.E. *ceorl*), who, according to the earliest law codes, could carry weapons and participate in public assemblies (O.E. *þing*) and other "public rituals" (Higham and Ryan 108).

Exhibiting many of the values and customs of early Germanic society in general, the society "was also largely structured around warfare" (Higham and Ryan 102). The agonistic struggle between kin groups for resources could break out in a feud between kindreds and their households. Out of the mechanism of tribal warfare arose the necessity for leaders to tie themselves to a Warband, "provid[ing] the second major organ of society" (102), Higham and Ryan argue, and the leader solidified his dominant position as a patron of a Warband through the ritualized and quasi-religious practice of gift-giving. The leader of a Warband was the "ring-giver" (O.E. *bēahgifa*), and therefore, bound his warriors to himself through the bestowing of rings.

Besides ceorl, Old English also had the term *frēa*, which "can denote the lord of a household" (Higham and Ryan 103), and the dependents (i.e., slaves or servants) who dwelt and worked on his property. Frēa carries the same weight as "chieftain" and even, as Higham and Ryan conjecture, "king." There is also the term *dryhten,* used in *Beowulf,* the longest example of Old English poetry, which means a "war leader," and therefore, also a "king." However, the word *cyning* (containing the O.E. word *cyn* for kin), from which the Modern English "king" is derived, won out as the "popular term" and "denoted small-scale kingship in early England" (Higham and Ryan 103). In other words, landowning warriors, who bound other warriors to themselves through gift-giving and tribal warfare, established themselves as the leading members of the early stages of Anglo-Saxon society, and it is this tribal chieftainship from which the later notion of kingship and the larger kingdoms bloomed.

It is conjectured that the Anglo-Saxon lords ruled over a mixed group of people, comprised of Anglo-Saxon newcomers and British natives: "No one believes nowadays that all the British (the indigenous population of Britain) were pushed westwards [sic] by the Angle and Saxon settlers, for it is perfectly clear from seventh-century and even some later texts that a Brittonic language was still being spoken in parts of midland and eastern England long after the English settlement."

(Davies 235).

For example, several early Anglo-Saxon rulers had names that where British in origin, such as Penda, king of Mercia (*c.* 632-55) (Higham and Ryan 178) and Cerdic, king of Wessex and ruler of Gewisse (d. 534), from whom many of the later kings of Wessex descended. Cerdic's name is specifically "derived from the Brittonic name *Caraticos*" (Davis 2010b). Further, Penda's name is quite possibly the curious result of the cultural mixing of Britons and Anglo-Saxons, as the kingdom of Mercia was comprised of Britain's midlands where, as stated above, some form of Britonnic was being spoken. Mercia also derives its name (from Old English *Mierce* "border") from its identity as a border kingdom, a buffer zone between the Welsh kingdoms to the west and the Anglo-Saxon kingdoms to the east (Foot). The fact that there was a strong enough British presence in the early Anglo-Saxon kingdoms to result in people as prestigious as kings bearing Britonnic names begs the question: what happened to the Britons, and where did they go?

The largest issue when answering that question is that the Britons are, unfortunately, largely archaeologically and culturally invisible: "Whatever it meant exactly to be *wealh* (literally, a foreigner, slave or Briton) in early Anglo-Saxon England, it was clearly a disadvantage; it may be that many British families sought to conceal their ancestry by adopting an "orthodox" Anglo-Saxon burial rite in order to improve their social status and economic conditions." (Hamerow 266).

In the law codes of Ine of Wessex, *weallas*—or Britons—were valued at half the *wergild* of an Englishman, "and a number of clauses [in the laws] suggest that most Britons possessed low legal status" (Hamerow 266). *Wergild*, literally meaning "man-payment" in Old English, was "the legal value set on a person's life," and therefore, the sum required for a dead man's family in order to "pay off the feud" (Lapidge 489). In other words, it was cheaper to kill a Briton than an Anglo-Saxon under Ine's law codes. It is believed that, as a result of the legal and cultural stigma against Britons in Anglo-Saxon society, Britons were prompted to conceal their identity as Britons, rapidly assimilate into English culture, and adopt Old English (Lapidge 266). Therefore, the development of early Anglo-Saxon society is less the story of a large invasion of North Sea Germanic people's driving out native Britons to Wales and Britany (although it was the case that British nobles relocated to Britany, France, and places as far as northwestern Spain) (Davies 236-237) and more the story of a small-scale migration of warriors who established their own chieftainships. These chieftainships then became powerful and prestigious enough for the Britons in their kingdoms to assimilate into their cultures, thereby disappearing from the record.

While the kingdoms of Kent, East and Middle Anglia, Lindsey, Deira, Bernicia, Mercia, Sussex, Wessex, and Essex claim the spotlight in the 7th- and 8th-century sources, "there were several smaller kingdoms," such as Gewisse or Hwicce, that should not be forgotten (Hamerow 280). The "fluid nature of early Anglo-Saxon social structure" allowed more powerful lords to incorporate the territories of the less powerful (Hamerow 281). The peculiar term, *bretwalda*, preserved in Bede and the *Anglo-Saxon Chronicle* sheds some light on the nature of kingdom formation.

The *Chronicle* used the term bretwalda to denote "a powerful king who dominated neighboring kings" (Bruce). Bede interpreted this term in Latin as *imperium*, the word originally used in Classical Latin to mean the power to command, but its meaning had broadened by Bede's time to mean "rule over more than one realm" (M. Wood). Bede explicitly listed seven kings who held imperium and were bretwaldas: Ælle of Sussex (*c.* 490), Ceawlin of Wessex (*c.* 590), Æthelbert of Kent (*c.* 600), Rædwald of East Anglia (617-*c.* 624), and Edwin, Oswald, and Oswiu of Northumbria (M. Wood 63).

The *Chronicle* later listed King Ecgberht of Wessex as bretwalda (Bruce). The key idea on Bede's list and in his rendering of bretwalda as imperium lies in his misunderstanding of the word in his day.

The word's older 7th-century form, *brytenwealda*, meant "wide ruler," as in a king who could exercise his rule and influence over his neighbors. However, Bede understood it to mean "Britain-ruler," and therefore, a king who dominated *all* Anglo-Saxon kingdoms, and by extension, *all* of Britain (Wood 63-64). Whatever the word's origin, the older brytenwealda is telling, concerning the nature of how the larger kingdoms, such as Wessex and Mercia, arose. A leading theory is that the emergence of kingdoms in the 6th century was the result of "competition" between chieftains for the influence typical of a "wide-ruler":

> This has given rise to the hypothesis that the major kingdoms of the mid[-]Saxon period (*c.*650-*c.*850) were the outcome of intense competition[s] between many much smaller polities in the sixth century, the more successful groups defeating and absorbing the less successful, culminating in the seventh century in a small number of dynasties with supra-regional authority. (Hamerow 282)

In other words, larger kingdoms emerged and solidified themselves by gobbling up and absorbing the smaller ones.

Early on, two of the most powerful kingdoms were Kent and East Anglia. In the 7th century, when Kent and East Anglia rose to prominence under their respective *bretwaldas*, the aforementioned Æthelberht and Rædwald, Britain was divided into an array of small kingdoms and polities (see map). The Britons—now the Welsh—were consolidated into an array of kingdoms in modern Wales: Gwynedd, Dyfed, Powys, Gwent, and Glywysing, with the first two (Gwynedd and Dyfed) being the major powers. There were also several British kingdoms in the north of Britain, Rheged, Strathclyde (Ystrad Clud), and Gododdin for a time, but these declined, with Rheged disappearing by 600 and Gododdin lingering until the 630s at the latest (Davies 246-248; Thacker 463). These northern kingdoms were the subject of several early Welsh poems, the most famous being *Y Gododdin*. This battle poem, supposedly composed by semi-legendary poet Aneirin, tells the story of a few hundred warriors from Gododdin, riding to the defense of the kingdom of Rheged, under attack by Northumbrians from Bernicia. The poem describes the feats of individual warriors and their glorious and noble defeat at the hands of the Bernicians (Aneirin xiii -xxix). Other British kingdoms in this century were being absorbed into Anglo-Saxon entities: Dumnonia, "the largest of British kingdoms" (Thacker 463) into the kingdom of Wessex, and Elmet into Northumbria through conquest "before the mid[-]seventh century" (Thacker 463).

The political fluidity and instability characteristic of Britain at the time enabled kings to exert themselves over their neighbors through various means. Kent was one of the earliest kingdoms to exploit this. The Jutes of Kent, claiming descent from the legendary Hengest and Horsa and further back to the Pagan god Woden (Higham and Ryan 72-74), occupied an advantageous position close to the goings-on of continental Europe. This resulted in Kent being the staging point for the introduction of Christianity to the then-Pagan Anglo-Saxons (more of this later).

Additionally, Kent's proximity to the prestigious Frankish kingdom, then ruled by the Merovingians, applied further cultural and religious pressure as several Pagan Kentish kings married Christian Frankish nobles, and Frankish styles of dress and metalwork were adopted there. The Kingston Brooch is an example of Kentish jewelry fashioned with a Merovingian influence. The *bretwalda* Æthelbehrt was married between 575-81 to Bertha, daughter of Frankish King Charibert, "when he was still only 'the son of a certain king in Kent,' as Gregory of Tours put in" (Higham and Ryan 148). Æthlberht's son, Ealdbald, also married a Frank, Emma of Neustrian origin, and afterward, many members of the Kentish royal family bore Frankish names such as Ealdbald's son Earconberht (640-664) (Thacker 473). Some have suggested that the presence of the Frankish style and culture alongside intermarriage between the two realms was "an expression of Merovingian [Frankish] overlordship" (Thacker 473). Certainly, the Frankish kings might have, for a time, thought of Kent as a client state.

It was under kings like Æthelberht where real social change occured among the Anglo-Saxon elites. Through the cultural influence of the prestigious Franks, the English began to adopt concepts of continental monarchy modeled after the style of Roman rule. This led English kings to style themselves as Christian kings instead of Pagan tribal chieftains (Higham and Ryan 163-165). However, this change was by far not consistent, and the Christianization of the Anglo-Saxon elite stagnated at the death of Æthelberht in 616:

> Kent, however, suffered in the political and religious divisions which followed Æthelberht's death, and by the 620s the overlordship had passed to Rædwald, king of the East Angles (d. 616 × 627), who maintained altars to both the old gods and the new. The wealth and power of the East Anglian political establishment is reflected in the royal tombs at the burial ground of Sutton Hoo, above all in the celebrated finds from the ship burial in Mound One. (Thacker 465)

Christianity also served as a useful mechanism for kings to exploit in the subordination of their rivals.

For example, King Oswald acted as godfather at the baptism of the West Saxon King Cynegils, whose daughter he had just married, thereby underlining his superior status. Æthelberht probably had a comparable role when King Rædwald was baptised [sic] at the Kentish court, and this was certainly the position taken by Oswiu at the baptisms of several subordinate kings conducted deep inside Northumbria. (Higham and Ryan 157)

This leaves room for the interpretive narrative that the death of Æthelberht allowed his most powerful rival, Rædwald, to apostatize in the absence of Kent's religious pressure and seize his place as bretwalda.

King Rædwald of East Anglia is most often identified as the man buried in the famous Sutton Hoo ship burial, discovered in the 1930s near Snape in Suffolk. The ship, measuring at 27 meters long, "contained the greatest burial hoard ever discovered in Britain," now on display in the British Museum (Higham and Ryan 133). The burial goods were found in a "timber chamber" inside the ship, and they included "precious weapons" (especially a sword, which was a display of wealth and status at the time), a "unique" coat of mail and helmet (possibly the most famous and identifiable find), the remains of a shield, the remains of a harp, "a purse containing Frankish coins," gaming pieces, drinking horns, and "silver table vessels" (Higham and Ryan 133). The reason many have claimed the burial belonged to King Rædwald is based partly on the wealth of the burial since it could be argued that such opulence is characteristic of a bretwalda. This would suggest Rædwald since he was the only East Anglian to be recognized as an over-king by Anglo-Saxon sources. Further, the coins would affirm the burial's association with Rædwald since they "are consistent with a date in the 620s when he is thought to have died" (Higham and Ryan 133).

It is, however, incredibly contentious whether Rædwald was actually *buried* in the burial, since no actual human remains have been found in the ship or its timber chamber, "either cremated or inhumed" as of yet (according to Guy's Hospital, London, around 1979). In 1975, the British Museum declared that there must have been a body where the arms and armor and other goods were found. It is conjectured that the reason no body or remains are identifiable in the burial is due to the acidic sand in which the ship was buried, which "could have eliminated all traces of a body, including teeth" (Wood 66). The mystery surrounding the body has led to the emergence of two theories.

The Sutton Hoo Helmet

The Sutton Hoo original shield fitting reconstructed on a modern frame

The first is that there *was* a body deposited with the goods, and all remains of it have been worn away, leaving a large space among the goods around the size of a human body. The second is that Sutton Hoo is, instead, a cenotaph, a "sepulchral monument made for a person who has been buried elsewhere" (Wood 66). However, in 1979, it was discovered among the original excavator's notes from 1939 that iron coffin fittings were initially discovered. Further, the position in which these fittings were originally found "formed the rectangular outline of a wooden coffin into which the grave goods surrounding the 'body' are neatly fit" (Wood 67). The matter is seemingly up for debate, and new evidence is always being uncovered in the field of archaeology. Nevertheless, it is quite possible that Sutton Hoo was the final resting place of King Rædwald.

The burial did not occur in a vacuum, however, and other such ship burials have been found elsewhere in Britain. However, the kind of burial at Sutton Hoo, the "combination of rich burial in a chamber under a large barrow was something new," and may have been "triggered by Frankish" and Christian influence (Higham and Ryan 131). These burials might, therefore, have been a performative form of religious and cultural resistance.

For the last quarter of the 7th century, the Northumbrians flourished under the three bretwaldas Edwin, Oswald, and Oswiu. As was the case with Oswiu, Northumbria was central in resolving religious and political conflict between both Rome and Iona, as well as between Bishops.

Edwin's predecessor, Æthelfrith (d. 616), integrated the Northumbrian kingdoms of Deira and Bernicia into one, uniting Anglian lands north of the Humber under one ruler. Edwin, Æthelrith's conqueror, continued this union. It was to him that Bede attributed "rule over all four of the peoples of seventh-century Britain—the English, British, Picts, and Irish. Only Kent lay outside his power" (Thacker 465). The stability of a unified Northumbria was, however, thrown into jeopardy upon Edwin's death in 633, in a battle against Cædwalla of Gwynedd and Pagan Penda of Mercia. The kingdom was later restored under the Bernician overlordship of King Oswald, the second of Bede's Northumbrian bretwaldas. It was Oswald who "re-established Northumbrian supremacy in the south" and over the Britons, Picts, and Gaels to the north (Thacker 465). However, King Penda of Mercia once again proved to be the bane of the Northumbrian kings' southerly ambitions, as Oswald was defeated and killed at the Battle of Maserfelth (possibly located at Oswestry in Shropshire) in 642. Northumbria managed to recover under Oswiu (Bede's third Northumbrian bretwalda) once again. He managed to defeat and kill Penda at the Battle of Winwæd in 655, resulting in his takeover of "much of the Mercians' territory" (Thacker 466). He further subjugated the kingdom by setting up Penda's Christian son, Peada, as his client ruler. Oswiu was the last Northumbrian king to dominate the south of Britain.

Northumbria's position of dominance over Mercia—and to a greater extent, the southern Anglo-Saxon world—neared its end when the Mercians drove out the Northumbrians in 658, establishing Penda's other son, Wulfhere (d. 674). The Northumbrian dominance truly came to a close when Ecgfrith (670-685), "Oswiu's son and successor," died in battle against the Picts at Nechtansmere in 685, marking a clear halt in Anglo-Saxon military expansion against the insular Celts, as prior to that, the Anglo-Saxons had experienced unchecked victory against their neighbors (Thacker 465-466; Bragg 56:45).

The beginning of the supposed Mercian "supremacies," which dominated the 8th century and lasted into the 9th, was traditionally with Æthelbald (716-57), and this hegemony was later carried on by Offa (757-96) (Zimmerman). Æthelbald can lay claim to being the longest-reigning

Anglo-Saxon king, and Offa was also "among the longest" (Higham and Ryan 182). To put this into perspective, throughout the course of the consecutive reigns of Æthelbald and Offa, 12 Northumbrian kings ruled. This could be interpreted as owing to the Mercian kings' stable reigns. However, while Æthebald and Offa mark a traditional departure from Northumbrian to Mercian supremacy in the Anglo-Saxon world, other Mercian kings, such as Penda and Wulfhere, "exerted considerable influence over their neighbours [sic]," (Higham and Ryan 182) as was the case with Penda being a general thorn in the Northumbrians' side. Why historians do not credit Penda as the starting point of Mercian supremacy is partly the result of Bede, seeing as the "true extent of Mercian power in this period is probably obscured by [his] Northumbria-centred [sic] narrative" (Higham and Ryan 182).

Mercia's hegemonial position should be considered as it was different from its neighbors. The success of Mercia's kings was "due in large part to their ability to harness the changing economy…from the late seventh to mid-ninth centuries" (Higham and Ryan 181). They thrived on growing international trade focused in *emporia* in cities such as London and were also able to exploit advancements in agriculture and "market-oriented production," as well as the patronage of "rich and powerful monasteries [that] now commanded extensive landed resources" (Higham and Ryan 181).

An invaluable source for the structure of Mercia and its relationship with its neighbors (as well as a source for the political layout of the southern Anglo-Saxon England layout in general) is the *Tribal Hidage*. A document with doubtful origin and date, it is a land survey of all the Anglo-Saxon territories south of the Humber and divided everything into "a 'list' of thirty-four 'tribal' territories" (Keynes 21). It names different groups of people, many of them unidentifiable, and estimates their size in "hides," with one hide equaling around the amount of land that a family would inhabit. The *Hidage* begins with a survey of the land making up that belonging to the Mercians, listed as 30,000 hides. The land in question is most likely what is considered the Mercian heartland in the middle of the Trent Valley, encompassing places such as Tamworth, Lichfield, and Repton. The *Hidage* then lists several smaller people supposedly comprising those subordinate to Mercia. The largest of these was "the *W[r]ocen sætna* (in Wrekin, Shropshire), the *Westerna* (the "Westerners," probably in the vicinity of Hereford), the *Lindesfarona* (in Lindsey, within Hatfield Chase), and the "*Hwinca*" (presumably the Hwicce, in the Severn valley)," which are all "assessed at 7000 [sic] hides apiece" (Keynes 21). The other Anglo-Saxon kingdoms are not treated to such an in-depth breakdown and are merely listed with their total hides.[9]

This could be because the original composer of the document was ignorant of the subdivisions of the other kingdoms, which would suggest its place of origin being within Mercia. Further, in the past, many have suggested the text is a Mercian document, commissioned by a king to breakdown and list all of the said king's lands. Several names have been put forward, but Keynes suggests that it was composed in the time of King Wulfhere (c. 670), since the territory of Elmet

---

[9] The East Angles at 30,000 hides, the East Saxons at 7,000 hides, Kent at 15,000 hides, the South Saxons at 7,000 hides, and the West Saxons at 100,000 hides (Keynes 23).

is listed, and after that time, it changed hands from Mercia to Northumbria. However, it could have also been composed in the time of Æthelbald or Offa and represent the extent of Mercian supremacy over all Anglo-Saxon territories south of the Humber. Whatever its origin, what the *Tribal Hidage* shows us about Mercia (and perhaps other southern Anglo-Saxon kingdoms to an extent) is that a uniform Mercian identity did not exist. Rather, Mercia was made up of a wide array of different people retaining individual local identities. Additionally, the *Hidage* "suggests that the social composition of the political organism which historians recognize as the 'kingdom of Mercia' might have been quite distinctive" (Keynes 25). This document is key to understanding the socio-political structure of Mercia and how its kings understood themselves to rule over various people (Keynes 21-25).

When writing about King Æthelbald of Mercia, Bede called him "the 'overking' of England south of the Humber" (Higham and Ryan 183). Another attestation of Æthelbald's hegemony over his neighbors is the Ismere Diploma of 736, which calls him "king not only of the Mercians but also of all the provinces which are called by the general name 'South English' [Sutangli]" (Higham and Ryan 183). Æthelbald (and other Mercian kings) "derived [his] strength from the extension of their control over the peoples around them" (Keynes 27), like how the Tribal Hidage shows us how the Mercians were a loose confederacy of people under one king. The same principle that applied to the Mercian people seems to have been applied to their neighbors in the way kings like Æthelbald attempted to subordinate them.

It is difficult to find actual evidence of Æthelbald's authority over the other kingdoms beyond a nominal sense. Descending from a "distant branch of the royal family" and living in exile, Æthelbald seized power in Mercia after the death of Ceolred in 716. The power vacuum left with the death of Wihtred of Kent (c. 725) and abdication of Ine of Wessex (c. 726) enabled Æthelbald to rise to eminence (Keynes 28; Higham and Ryan 183). He was able to exercise "direct control over the *Hwicce*" (Higham and Ryan 194) and also the East Saxons (Keynes 30). His hold over Kent was tenuous, however. His "concern to foster his interests in Kent" is "well attested;" however, contemporary Kentish charters give no indication that their kings operated "under Mercian control" (Keynes 30). Æthelbald was more overtly successful against the West Saxons than Kent and managed to wrest through a conquest of West Saxon territory, clashing with King Cuthred of Wessex (r. 740-56) several times. Oddly, these kings are also attested to conducting a campaign together in 743 against the Welsh. There are additional attestations of Mercian raids in the Wye Valley (possibly a part of this joint West Saxon and Mercian campaign), and the 9th-century Pillar of Eliseg "records the Mercians being driven from Powys in the middle of the eighth century" (Higham and Ryan 185). These three sources could all be describing the same campaign in 743, but other than this, Æthelbald seems to have had no success in subduing the Welsh to the west. While, in the 740s, Boniface addressed Æthelbald in a letter as "wielding the glorious sceptre [sic] of imperial rule over the English," the only real direct rule Æthelbald secured outside of Mercia was over the *Hwicce*, Middlesex Essex (particularly London), and the parts of Wessex he conquered.

Æthelbald's rule is characterized by cruelty and "periodic violence lapsing into despotism." His long reign ended in 757 "when he was murdered—treacherously at night by his bodyguards" (Higham and Ryan 185-186). His eminent position set a precedent for his successor, Offa, who would go on to actualize many of his predecessor's southerly ambitions.

Upon his death, Æthelbald was succeeded by Beornred, who only ruled for a few months. Beornred's brief rule was wracked with civil war, and eventually, his kinsman Offa, a cousin of Æthelbald, drove him out and seized the throne (Higham and Ryan 186; Wood 80). Offa's reign was similar to Æthelbald's in several aspects, especially with respect to the geographical "concentration of his power" (Higham and Ryan 186). However, he was also significantly different from Æthelbald in that he "harness[ed] more fully the ideological apparatus offered by Christianity and the Church" and how he drew from models of Christian kingship, inspired partly by the style of rule characteristic of Charlemagne, the Carolingian emperor (r. 771-814) (Jotischky and Hull 26).

Offa managed to take Æthelbald's southerly ambitions further, greatly enlarging the kingdom of Mercia. In the 780s, he reinstated Mercian control over the Hwicce and South Saxons, ending their local "independent royal dynasties." He likewise managed to do so in Kent, which he treated differently from Sussex and the Hwicce. He seemed to prefer to maintain local elites and dynasties among the South Saxons and the Hwicce, making them "non-royal leaders" or ealdormen (Jotischky and Hull 187). He initially employed the same tactic in Kent in the 760s, when he subdued the kingdom but let the "local rulers retain their status as kings" (Keynes 30). This policy was short-lived, as Kent managed to break free "from Mercian overlordship in 776" (Keynes 30). When he regained control of Kent, Offa restrained the local king's authority and assumed direct control of the kingdom for the rest of his reign (Keynes 30). Offa also reasserted "Mercian authority over the Thames Valley," defeating the West Saxons in battle at Bensington in 779 and "subsequently gain[ing] control of territory on the south bank of the Avon" (Higham and Ryan 187). In this way, Offa reinstated Mercian rule in the territories to which Æthelbald had first extended his authority.

Offa managed to spread his influence farther outside Mercia's territory. Coins minted in East Anglia bearing his name suggest they came "under Offa's authority" in the 790s. Further, Offa ordered King Æthelberht of East Anglia to be beheaded in 794, possibly in a crack-down on local elites and political enemies. During Offa's reign, as it was during Æthelbald's, Mercia retained its control of London and Middlesex, even though Offa "does not appear to have exercised any authority in the East Saxon kingdom itself" (Higham and Ryan 187). Offa also extended his influence through political marriages. Though he had clashed with the West Saxons under King Cynewulf in his conquest of parts of Wessex, his relationship with his southern neighbors "seemed to be more cordial" during the reign of King Beorhtric (r. 786-802), to whom he married his daughter Eadburh (Higham and Ryan 187). He also married his daughter, Ælfflæd, to King Æthelred of Northumbria in 792, "but this may have been the limit of Offa's involvement" in Northumbrian affairs, as that kingdom was experiencing an intense period of political and dynastic turmoil (Higham and Ryan 187).

Compared to Æthelbald, Offa ruled an exceptionally larger kingdom: "By the final decades of his reign, Offa had become the ruler of a kingdom stretching from the Midlands down to the south-east [sic] coast—a vast territory by Anglo-Saxon standards. That Offa and those around him conceived of this territory as a uniform kingdom, an enlarged Mercia, is clear. In his charters and on his coinage he appears, almost without exception, simply as the king of the Mercians, adopting no grander or more expansive royal style." (Higham and Ryan 187).

This kingdom drew the praise of many, such as Alcuin, Emperor Charlemagne's Northumbrian scholar and advisor, who praised Offa as "the glory of Britain, the trumpet of proclamation, the sword against foes, the shield against enemies" (Keynes 29). While such praise would suggest another bretwalda, it is important to remember not only that such "grandiose styles and naturally exaggerated forms of expression are not always reliable indicators of historical truth" but also that Offa was merely interested in advancing Mercia's interests and authority and not that of a united English kingdom (Higham and Ryan 187).

What Offa is perhaps most known for is the dyke bearing his name. Offa's Dyke is a large manmade earthwork running along the border between the then kingdoms of Mercia in England and Powys in Wales. You can still visit parts of it today in places such as Clun or Edenhope Hill in Shropshire. Writing in the late 9th century, Welsh cleric Asser said that Offa "had a great a dyke built between Wales and Mercia from sea to sea" (Higham and Ryan 188), but it is unclear exactly how far the original earthwork stretched. David Hill "in the 1970s-1990s suggested that it extended only from Treuddyn in the north to Rushock Hill in the south" at merely around 100 kilometers (around 62 miles); however, other claims reckon it to be around 240 kilometers (150 miles) (Wood 78). Later claims have suggested that it ran "as far south as Sedbury Cliffs in Gloucestershire," but it is probable that it did *not* run as far as the sea in the north. Its construction must have been quite the undertaking, taking as many as 5,000 to 125,000 men to build (Higham and Ryan 188) and requiring "smiths from Gloucester" and "quarrymen and masons from Northamptonshire" (Wood 77). Its exact purpose is less certain. It is generally agreed that Offa's Dyke marked a line of demarcation between Mercia and "the newly resurgent Powys" (Higham and Ryan 188). This was nothing new in early medieval Britain, as various earthworks, such as Wansdyke, constructed by Britons to separate their kingdoms from the newly settled Saxons in the Thames Valley ("The 'Walls of Severus'"), had been built before. Further, it was seemingly constructed to hinder Welsh "cattle rustlers and small-scale raiding parties" by limiting the ease of transit between the two realms. It also played into Offa's kingly and powerful image: "The Dyke must also have been a powerful ideological statement, inviting comparisons between Offa and Roman rulers of the past who had undertaken similarly grand construction projects—the Hadrianic and Antonine Walls being the most obvious insular examples." (Higham and Ryan 188).

While it has been challenged whether the dyke can actually be attributed to Offa (the most controversial recent argument being that it was built by Roman Emperor Septimus Severus) ("The 'Wall of Severus'"), the general consensus still holds that Offa did indeed build Offa's Dyke and that it established a clear frontier between Mercia and Powys, as well as being a distinct show of might and power to his Welsh neighbors (Keynes 31).

Outside of Britain, Offa shared an interesting relationship with Charlemagne, one that informs us of how he viewed himself and his kingship. Offa seems to have aspired to emulate the same status and image of that of Emperor Charlemagne in several ways, even reaching "an equality" with him (Higham and Ryan 189). Anglo-Saxon kings drawing inspiration from Frankish culture is not unprecedented, as was seen with Kent and East Anglia. It does *not*, however, seem to be that Charlemagne felt as if he and Offa were equals, and at times, he perhaps viewed Offa as his subordinate. For example, the Frankish emperor sought Offa's daughter's hand in marriage for his son, Charles. However, when Offa "demanded reciprocal marriage" where Charlemagne's daughter, Bertha, would marry his son, Ecgfrith, in return, Charlemagne was insulted and "imposed a trade embargo on English merchants in Francia" (Higham and Ryan 189). The message in Charlemagne's response was clear: the two monarchs were not equals in his eyes. Further, when trade between the two peoples was eventually resumed in the 790s, Charlemagne, in his letters, was always "by the grace of God, king of the Franks and Lombards and Patrician of the Romans," but Offa was merely "King of the Mercians" (qtd. in Higham and Ryan 189). The point was that Charlemagne, ruling over many groups of people, had greater influence and power than Offa, who ruled over one.

The best example of what Charlemagne thought of Offa was his gift of a "Hunnish" sword to Offa. The weapon, selected from the spoils of war in Charlemagne's conquest against the Avars in Pannonia (modern-day Hungary), was, no doubt, a kingly and "prestigious" gift. Yet this gift, no matter how lavish, was part of a broader hierarchy of gift-giving, where the gift was a signal of the transaction between the empowered giver and the subservient receiver (Higham and Ryan 189). In other words, Charlemagne's gift to Offa was one that a lord would give a retainer or subordinate (think of the relationship the aforementioned Anglo-Saxon *bēahgifa* or *frēa* had with the retainers in his Warband). This reflects Charlemagne's attitudes toward the rest of the spoils taken from the same campaign against the Avars, where he readily dispensed plunder among his "leading churchmen and nobility as well as other faithful men" (Higham and Ryan 189). It is possible that, despite how Offa viewed his relationship with Charlemagne, the Frankish emperor might have thought of the Mercian king as his "man" in the Anglo-Saxon sphere, a subordinate.

Offa was not the first to exploit the apparatus of Christianity and integrate it into his blueprint for kingship, but he does represent a significant shift toward a style of kingship that was different from the tribalism of the 7th century. He was inspired by continental Frankish models. Part of this was how he quite consciously distanced himself from his predecessor, Æthelbald, who was famed for his rejection of monogamy and Christian sexual standards. He was able to do this through the coins that were minted bearing his image. While being a way of emulating the Roman Emperors who also minted coins bearing their images, coins were also a way for Offa to keep himself in the public image, reminding his subjects who their king was. Since coins were a fundamentally public and conspicuous way of broadcasting his image to his people, Offa could integrate signals of his monogamy and sexual purity by placing his queen, Cynethryth, in the limelight. Coins were minted bearing her image and name, and in royal charters, she was called "Queen of the Mercians," which "no doubt reflected her importance at court" (Higham and Ryan

181). The significance of accenting Cynethryth's position in court and governance was that it strengthened the image of the royal family and "stressed the legitimacy of her union with Offa," and by extension, the legitimacy of their children (Higham and Ryan 191).

A coin bearing the image of Queen Cynefrith of Mercia, minted by the "moneyer Eoba" (Higham and Ryan 191)

Offa tried quite hard to solidify a dynasty and secure a smooth and indisputable succession for his son, Ecgfrith, but this was not without bloodshed and "strategies perhaps less becoming of a pious king" (Higham and Ryan 192). As Alcuin wrote, "How much blood the father shed to secure the kingdom for his son" (Higham and Ryan 191). When Offa died of natural causes in 796 and his son succeeded him, Ecgfrith only reigned for a few months until his natural death in December of the same year. Ecgfrith's successor, King Coenwulf (r. 796-821), was, by no means, less magnificent than Offa. He ruled over many of the same territories Offa had managed to subdue, and he even expanded Mercia's lands, successfully subduing the kingdom of Essex. However, it was in Coenwulf's reign that Mercia experienced real competition and impediments to its authority in the way of Wessex: "The death of King Beorhtric of Wessex in 802 and the succession of the previously exiled Ecgberht (r. 802–39) marked the beginnings of a reversal in the fortunes of Mercia and Wessex, a shift adumbrated by an unsuccessful Mercian raid into West Saxon territory in the immediate aftermath of Ecgberht's accession." (Higham and Ryan 192)

After Offa and Coenwulf, Wessex rose to eminence in Anglo-Saxon England in Ecgbert, his son Æthelwulf, and especially his grandson, the famous Ælfred the Great.

The Rise of Wessex

It was during the reign of King Cenwulf of Mercia (r. 796-821) that Mercia's "supremacies" began to wane. Cenwulf's reign is by no means any less noteworthy than those of Æthelbald and Offa. He can even be credited with extending his kingdom's influence and authority further. For example, he successfully subdued the kingdom of Essex "with the East Saxon King Sigered (c.

798-825) witnessing Cenwulf's charters first as king, then as sub-king simply as an ealdorman" (Higham and Ryan 191). Later, he was able to dominate East Anglia and Kent as his predecessors had. However, Cenwulf's reign experienced "the problems and tensions that seem ultimately to have undermined Mercian hegemony south of the Humber," leading to the rise of Wessex (Higham and Ryan 192). Cenwulf's death in 821 certainly marked the end of nearly a century of Mercian hegemony south of the Humber (Higham and Ryan 192).

Mercia's rival Wessex rose to take its place, and the 9th century would prove disastrous, with it being partitioned both by Wessex and the invading Norsemen. The reign of Cenwulf's brother Ceolwulf (r. 821-3) (Keynes *Coenwulf* 115) was "short-lived and ended badly" with the *Anglo-Saxon Chronicle* mentioning that "he was deprived of the kingdom in 823" (Keynes 239). Mercia's power and authority were further crippled by the killing of Ealdormen Burghelm and Muca, who were dominant figures in "Ceolwulf's regime" (Keynes 239). Mercia's grip on its tributary kingdoms weakened, and the once-great kingdom lost them to Wessex, now ruled by the once-exiled King Ecgberht.

King Ecgberht of Wessex (r. 802-39) was instrumental in Mercia's decline and Wessex's rise in the 9th century. Ecgberht, the grandfather of the famous King Ælfred the Great, "claimed descent from King Ine's brother Ingeld, and his father Ealhmund may have briefly been king in Kent in 784" (York, *Ecgberht, King of Wessex* 162). In 786, he attempted to take the throne of Wessex, but was expelled from the country (York, *Ecgberht, King of Wessex* 162). Afterward, he lived in exile at the court of Emperor Chárlemagne until he ascended to the West Saxon throne in 802 (York, *Ecgberht, King of Wessex* 162).

In 825, the East Anglians appealed to the king of Wessex "for peace and protection," suggesting that that kingdom came under Wessex's dominion (Higham and Ryan 240). Later in the same year, the West Saxons under Ecgberht defeated the Mercians at the Battle of Ellendun (now Wroughton in Wiltshire), resulting in Kent, Surrey, Sussex, and Essex coming under Wessex's control (Yorke *Ecgberht, King of Wessex* 162; Keynes *England, 700-900* 37). Within the same year, the East Angles "killed Ceolwulf's successor, Beornwulf" (Higham and Ryan 240). Mercia simply did not recover after Cenwulf's death, and Ceolwulf's removal proved disastrous, as the kingdom could not reinvigorate its hold on its tributaries quickly enough before Wessex snatched them up from under them. For Mercia, it was a period of political upheaval (Keynes *England, 700-900* 37).

Ecgberht pushed his ambitions further, and in 829, he conquered Mercia, according to the *Anglo-Saxon Chronicle*, which subsequently added him to Bede's list of *bretwaldas*. He supposedly went on to accept the "submission of Northumbria" as well, effectively exerting influence over all Anglo-Saxon kingdoms (Yorke *Ecgberht, King of Wessex* 162). Exactly how much control Ecgberht had over all the kingdoms is murky, and Northumbria's submission could have been strictly nominal. Further, the *Anglo-Saxon Chronicle*, considering the nature of its composition, held a West Saxon bias (see discussion below), and its willingness to list Ecgberht but not Kings Æthelbald or Offa of Mercia as *bretwalda* could be the intentional or unintentional work of an "anti-Mercian" bias (Keynes *England, 700-900* 39).

Ecgberht only ruled Mercia for one year, however, and the *Chronicle* states that in 830, a certain Wiglaf (d. 839) ascended to Mercia's throne. It is not clear whether Ecgberht willingly or unwillingly gave up the Mercian throne, but the kingdoms did not share any "residual antagonism" afterward (Keynes *England, 700-900* 41).

Ecgberht's policies and style of rule set him apart from previous dominating kings like Offa, especially in how he treated subordinate kingdoms. While the Mercians preferred to rule things from a distance, Ecgberht was much more hands-on, especially in Kent, where he had personal dynastic interests and claim (as his father was supposedly king there). He made an effort to make regular visits to Kent, and he was "careful to cultivate support in the locality" (Keynes *England, 700-900* 40). Overall, it seems that Ecgberht, his successor, and son, Æthelwulf, respected "the separate identity of Kent and its associated provinces" (Keynes *England, 700-900* 40). In sum, he styled his rule as that of a "bipartite kingdom" of Wessex and Kent, stretching across southern England. Additionally, he worked hard to foster a strong military and dynastic alliance with Mercia, which, in the 9th century, may have been wracked with dynastic competition between two different dynasties, labeled as the B and C dynasties. There was, however, another element to the reigns of Ecgberht and his successor's: they consistently found themselves clashing with the Vikings on multiple occasions, who, in 793, made a sudden and bombastic entrance into the course of Anglo-Saxon history (Keynes *England, 700-900* 41; Higham and Ryan 240; Yorke *Ecgberht, King of Wessex* 162).

The Viking Raids

According to the *Anglo-Saxon Chronicle*, shortly before the first major Viking raid in England, "Danish men" arrived during King Brihtric's rule in Wessex. Three ships had come to Portland Island, and when the king's men rode down to greet the anticipated merchants, they were murdered. Just a few years later, different sources speak of King Offa of Mercia and Charlemagne himself already taking actions to fortify coastal defenses against seafaring pagans, most likely referring to the Vikings.

The most renowned of the first raids against a foreign target by Scandinavian Vikings took place in 793, on the east coast of England, at the monastery of Lindisfarne. The events surrounding the attack were written down by the terror filled monks and scribes inhabiting the monastery, who very vividly described the violence taking place. According to the Christian ecclesiastic Alcuin of York, who lived at the time of the event, the raid came as a complete surprise. He described the church of St. Cuthbert as "spattered with the blood of priests of God, stripped of all its furnishings, exposed to the plundering of pagans - a place more sacred than any in Britain." A year later the Vikings, as recorded in a contemporary document, "ravaged in Northumbria, and plundered Ecgfrith's monastery at Donemuthan," and in 800 "the most impious armies of the pagans cruelly despoiled the church of Hartness and Tynemouth, and returned with (their) plunder to the ships".

The attack on Lindisfarne was, from the victims' perspectives, the culmination of a series of bad omens from God himself, as depicted in the *Anglo-Saxon Chronicle*. After whirlwinds, flashes of lightning and famine, the heathens came to slaughter, plunder and ravage the church of God at Lindisfarne. The explanation was simply that they were sent as a punishment from God, and that the monks at the monastery surely must have done something terrible to anger him in this manner. The Vikings, on the other hand, held a more down-to-earth or pragmatic view of the incident and explained it with quite a different background. They had heard of the monastery long before plundering it, with all its riches hidden away from earthly eyes, after several trade contacts with the kingdom of Northumbria where it was located. The Vikings knew that the monastery had been built a rather far distance from the closest town of York and picked it for its many weaknesses.

The large increase of trade in the area had made a significant contribution to the economy of the monastery, making it a particularly wealthy outpost. The target more or less presented itself, and the Vikings already knew to wait for the tide, making the docking easy and at the same time cutting the monastery off from the lands and roads leading to it, leaving it without any possibility of being aided. The location of the monastery had been chosen, ironically, simply because it was so isolated and hard to access from land. Anyone wanting to visit – or plunder – the monastery would be spotted and heard of long before they arrived. No one in the monastery had predicted a ship arriving in the shallow waters, coming from way across the seas. This element of surprise was to become the Vikings' hallmark.

The fact that the first large-scale attack was aimed at a monastery contributed to their image of being cruel and ferocious. Monks and priests had of course seen war and conflicts before, mainly between their warring kings and leaders, but Christian armies usually left sacred churches and monasteries alone, even in enemy territories. The Vikings had no sentiment or fear of the Christian God, merely a desire for the riches dwelling in these religious houses, and though the Vikings couldn't have known it, Lindisfarne was located in the political heartland of the north and was an important symbol of Christianity in England. It was here that an exquisite work, the *Lindisfarne Gospel*, had been created hundreds of years earlier. Bound in leather and studded with jewels, it was a treasure to the Anglo-Saxon world.

Though all this made Lindisfarne such a holy place, the books, saints and prayers could not help the monks residing in Lindisfarne monastery when the Vikings suddenly decided to attack. The rumors of the attack spread quickly and gave the Vikings a particularly bad reputation - not only had they attacked a house of God and stolen from it, they had also destroyed holy relics, killed monks, and abducted some of them for slavery. No stories from the eyewitnesses have survived, and nobody is entirely sure how true the accounts are, but there is a stone in the vicinity of the monastery probably was constructed about a year later to honor the dead, and it depicts violent assailants and praying monks.

The Yorkish monk Alcuin is responsible for writing the records mostly used when examining the sack of Lindisfarne, though he was not present at the time of the incident, and he had strong incentives to strengthen the political position of the church, which is important to keep in mind when reading his work. He also knew some of the monks and the bishop at the monastery, obviously making it hard for him to remain impartial. His records include some grave exaggerations, but even so, the image of the Vikings' actions in Lindisfarne in 793 rests in stark contrast to the previously peaceful trade interactions. The attackers consisted of a relatively small fleet, probably some three or four breakaway ships from a larger fleet heading towards Scotland the same year. The plunder of Lindisfarne, as well as the raids in Scotland, met little resistance, so bands of Vikings kept returning to them both for a few years.

The second reported attack on another monastery in England took place in Northumbria a few years after 793. The Donemuthan monastery was raided under similar crude circumstances as Lindisfarne was, and these Viking bands are thought to have come from Norway, albeit some of the records talk of them as Danes. After these two initial attacks on the two English kingdoms, there are no further records of any raids towards England for nearly four decades and the general conception is that the Vikings found better raiding opportunities in Scotland and went on to plunder the Hebrides for a few years. It is highly probable that the band of Vikings attacking Scotland was based on the Orkney Isles, making it easier to spread their raids and come back more frequently. Shortly after that, they moved on to also raid Ireland, which at the time suffered from political disarray and could not muster up must resistance to the raids.

In England things quieted down until a new wave of Viking activity was noted in southern England, on the Isle of Sheppey. In 835, the Viking phenomenon was a fact, and their activity did not just increase in the British Isles and Ireland, they also started to appear more frequently on the continent, becoming a nuisance to the Carolingian Empire. This is when the real beginning of 200 years of Viking raids actually kicked off, mainly driven by the Danes. The Anglo-Saxon Chronicle tells of raids on a yearly basis, and we can follow the traces of the Vikings thanks to this well-kept record. Due to the political turmoil in both England and Frankia, many more records were written at the time, also including the Vikings in the stories.

Attacks frequently happened in areas bordering between two kingdoms, but in those cases, the belligerents were often seen coming from far away and most villages had time to plan their defenses, hide their valuables, and evacuate the non-fighting citizens. The Vikings gave no window for escape thanks to their quick movements, and their attacks might've been described as unusually ferocious simply because the element of surprise gave them the upper hand. They could easily fight against unprepared farmers, and their strategies didn't require much finesse. The early Vikings were probably not particularly good with swords or axes, relying more on brute strength than technique, but tactics would develop later when attempts were made conquering larger cities, like the famous attacks on Paris where the Vikings worked with a number of different strategies.

The height of the Viking Age would also be defined by the political instability following the fall of the Carolingians in France by the mid-9th century, the competition between the English kings, and the not yet stabilized Russia in the east. The Vikings used the commotion to their advantage and in some cases formed alliances with warring tribes, kings, and chieftains on the continent, all the while attacking weaker villages and towns neglected by authorities. Rumors of fast loot, easy targets, and the spirit of adventure soon spread over Scandinavia and provided incentive for many young men to leave on one of the Viking trips.

The sense of adventure is often neglected when discussing the reasons for these sudden raids across the seas, but returning Vikings and the poems dedicated to them had a way of glorifying and endorsing the trips as something much more glorious than they actually turned out to be. Many young men would be lured to prove their strength on the battlefield rather than face the rough soils and hostile climate in Scandinavia.

Though the sources are biased, it is safe to say these were different types of attacks, and not just a more persuasive form of trade. The way in which the attacks were carried out, the swiftness of them, and the raw plunder and looting makes them the first of their kind, and historians can classify it as the first of the attacks usually associated with the Vikings. After a hundred years of accumulation and centralisation of wealth, the seafaring Scandinavians knew very well that there was plenty of goods to plunder all along the coastlines of Britain and mainland Europe. To plunder would be much easier than to establish new trade routes, necessitating a crew and the ability to build a network for pocketing some of the profits. The system had already been stabilized and was set around a number of craftsmen, merchants, sailors, chieftains and kings, not letting new actors onto the stage. That is why the Vikings started arriving with weapons and seeking to loot and kill. Moreover, moving swiftly overseas instead of slowly over land gave the villagers and monks little or no time to prepare for an attack, and during these early attacks, they were often overrun while in the midst of daily life.

The classic portrait of the Viking is to a large extent exaggerated, but when the raids suddenly started, the reasons to fear them were in many cases justified. The end of the 8th century had clearly marked a difference in their behavior.

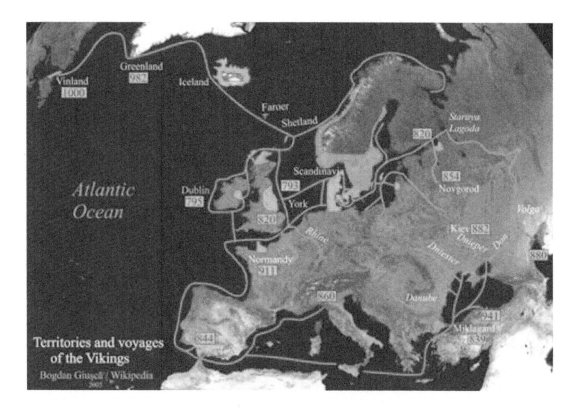

A map of Viking raiding throughout Europe

When people read about the Viking excursions on the North Sea and to the west, they mainly focus on the long and strenuous trips to the British kingdoms and what took place with the intrigues of the English kings like Ecbert, Aella and Offa. There are, however, other sides to the story of the Vikings in the west, and of their impact on the northern islands off the coast of Scotland. Evidence has been found that the Vikings made these their base for raiding Ireland and Scotland by expelling the original population. Many buildings were taken over and later modified to their own standards, and it is most likely that the Vikings either executed or enslaved the population. The local names of places and geographical sights, as well as the abundance of Viking graves and hoards, bear witness to the complete occupation by Scandinavians in Orkney and Shetland, and there is a reason why the Faroe Islands still belong to Denmark. Today almost none of the original Pictish names have survived, while the Scandinavian names are prevalent.

Later on, the Isle of Man and the Hebrides were colonized by the Vikings, but in the early days they mainly used Orkney and Shetland to launch attacks on Ireland and Scotland. The sources give a rough overview of the raids on Iona in 795, 802, and 806, proving how England was left alone for many years while the Vikings found it more convenient to settle on the northern islands and launch smaller raids on the Scottish and Irish coasts. Most of the routes from Orkney and Shetland heading west were dotted with islands and skerries, making it possible to stop, refill supplies, and wait out bad weather. The trip from Norway to Ireland could therefore be done quite easily in one season, while the summer was spent living on the isles.

The climate around these areas was to a large extent similar to the Scandinavian conditions, making it easy for the Vikings to adapt and settle. The main incentives, however, were the many and easily accessible riches in northern England, Scotland, and Ireland, which became some of the most important sources of income for the Vikings during the era. The Orkneys held an important strategic location and became the seat of a long dynasty of Norwegian-descended earls, although it is unclear at what point in history this was initiated. The most common conclusion is that the islands were taken over by the late 8th century, which correlates well with the years of the Scottish and Irish raids, as well as the absence of raids in England.

After a few decades of temporary dwellings, the Vikings settled permanently and established farms and proper villages all over the scattered islands off and along the Scottish coast. Still, the area remained rural and the main economic centers of the Vikings would be Dublin in Ireland and York in England, taken over by the Scandinavians later during the Viking Age.

The Great Army

The 840s and 850s saw a change in Viking raids. Scandinavians were getting bolder as their raids continued to increase in size. More importantly, they were beginning to stay. The trend of raids becoming larger was not isolated in England. For example, in 845, a Viking known only as Ragnar led a fleet of 120 ships up the Seine, smashed the army of Emperor Charles the Bald, raided Paris and the nearby monastery of Saint-Germain-des-Prés, and lastly, extorted a ransom of 7,000 pounds of silver from Charles (Haywood 152). When contrasted with the size of past attacks recorded in the sources—three ships in 789, 13 in 820, nine in 835, and either 25 or 35 in 836—this army is positively massive. Consider also that the standard ship the Vikings manned "could transport some thirty to forty men" (Coupland 194). At their largest, Viking armies could number in the thousands. In this period, Viking armies were also beginning to stay for longer when they raided. Gone were the days of lightning-fast hit-and-run raids at places like Lindisfarne. One version of the *Chronicle* says how the Vikings (c. 851) stayed on Thanet in Kent, and there, the "heathen[s,] for the first time[,] remained over winter" (Coupland 194; Keynes *Vikings in England* 52). This began a trend in raiding, where invading armies would settle for a time or even permanently. On top of Viking armies being larger and more willing to settle, they were also more active. The period of the 840s and 850s witnessed a significant ramping up of Viking activity, with seemingly more and more Scandinavians taking part in and forming various parties. Coincidentally, the best archetype for these new trends in Viking expeditions was instrumental in affecting English history in the 9th century: the Great Army (Coupland 194; Keynes *Vikings in England* 52).

In the year 865/66, a large "heathen army" of around 3,000 warriors landed in East Anglia, "established winter quarters[,] and procured horses there" (Sommerville 47). Later, they made peace with the East Anglians. This army would be instrumental in reshaping England, and over the course of roughly two decades, all the Anglo-Saxon kingdoms but Wessex had been destroyed or completely taken over (Keynes *Vikings in England* 51-52; Downham 342). The difference between this Viking army's expedition and previous ones like Lindisfarne was that they came seeking lands to conquer and settle (Higham and Ryan 259).

The exact nature of the army's composition and origin is a matter of debate. It is plausible—and it has been suggested—that the army originated in Scandinavia. It is unlikely the army was the doing of one man and made up of his own warriors, nor is it likely the soldiers all came from one specific place. The Great Army "appears to have been a loose confederation of groups [of Vikings] already operating in Britain, Ireland, and Francia[,] temporarily united in the pursuit of common goals" (Higham and Ryan 259). Therefore, the army's leadership might have been a patchwork of give-and-take cooperation among the various warlords who, each of them heading their own Warband, banded together to form a larger whole. Among them were characters such as Ívarr and his brother, Halfdan, who claimed to be the sons of legendary Ragnar Loðbrok, [10] "as well as another 'king' called *Bagsecg*, and several 'earls'" (Keynes *Vikings in England* 54).

The character of Ívarr has as intricate and colorful a background as his supposed father, Ragnar. Many have identified him as the legendary Ívarr the Boneless, according to Icelandic tradition. Further, it is possible that the Ívarr of the Great Army can be identified as King Ívarr I of Dublin (Ímhar in Irish and pronounced similarly) (d. 873), who was active in Ireland in the 850s and 860s (Keynes *Vikings in England* 54; Higham and Ryan 259). It is uncertain as to what extent these figures are related and if they are, indeed, the same person, but the possibility remains.

In 866, the army marched north to Northumbria, which, according to *Chronicle,* was in "a state of disunity and civil unrest," as the Northumbrians "deposed their king Osberht and replaced him with Ælla," who seems to have had "'no hereditary right' to the throne," though later sources claim that they were brothers (Higham and Ryan 270). The Vikings besieged and captured York and killed both Osberht and Ælla. Later, they moved around between Northumbria and Mercia in 867, back to Northumbria in 868, and then returned to Mercia and then East Anglia in 869. During this period, they were seemingly content to "allow the East Angles, the Northumbrians, and the Mercians to 'make peace' with them," that is, to let the Anglo-Saxon kingdoms pay them off with money or supplies. Besides killing both claimants to the Northumbrian throne, the Viking Army seemed to operate as past large Viking armies like Ragnar's at Paris had, that is, to exact tribute (Keynes *Vikings in England* 54; Higham and Ryan 260; Downham 342).

However, their tactics changed in 869 when they marched to East Anglia, killed the local King Edmund, and conquered the kingdom. The implication is that they "displaced the existing form of government" and "established themselves in direct control of the land" (Keynes *Vikings in England* 54). They might have also denigrated power to puppet monarchs named Æthelred and Oswald, though nothing but their names are known due to coinage from the time period. After

---

[10] Not much is known as to who this famous Ragnar was. Sources for him are all pseudo-historical and legendary: book nine of the 12th-century *Gesta Danorum* by Danish historian Saxo Grammaticus (c.1150- c.1220), the 12th-century Icelandic poem *Krákumál*, and the 13th-century Iceland *Ragnars saga loðbrókar* (Haywood 162). Attempts have been made to identify Ragnar with the Viking of the same name who raided Paris and exacted tribute from Charles the Bald in the 850s (as does Michael Hirst in the History Channel's *Vikings*), Danish King Reginfred (d. 814), and Ragnall, who was a Viking active in Ireland and Scotland in the 860s (152).

his death, King Edmund was later venerated as a saint and the Christianized Anglo-Danes who dwelt in East Anglia between c. 890-c. 910 minted coins with his image and saintly title on them. His martyrdom was the subject of several hagiographical manuscripts, such as *Lives of Saints* by Ælfric, abbot of Eynsham (c, 955-1010), where Edmund is depicted as a pacifistic martyr killed at the hands of bloodthirsty Pagans (Mostert 165-166). If the Ívarr of the Viking Army was the same Ímhar of Dublin, it seems that he departed from the Great Army for a time and was "active on both sides of the Irish Sea from 870 until his death in 873" (Keynes *Vikings in England* 54).

In 871, the Viking army was reinforced by another "Summer Army," led by Guthrum, Answend, and Oscetyl. This army met up with the Great Army near Reading, as in that year, they launched their first major offensive against Wessex, which led to the West Saxons' having to make peace, assumedly in the same fashion of ransom as had the other kingdoms. The army was later active in major settlements of "extended Mercia" (Keynes *Vikings in England* 54). London (871/2), Torksey (872/3), and Repton (873/4). Excavations at Repton have revealed an encampment along the River Trent, where the Viking possibly wintered. At that site, some 250 of their own were buried during the winter of 873/4. In 873/4, they returned to Mercia, drove King Burgred into exile, and set up a man named Ceolwulf as their puppet king in Burgred's place. After the toppling of Mercia, the army split into smaller contingents. Halfdan returned to Northumbria, and he and his men "shared out the land of the Northumbrians, and they proceeded to plough [sic] and to support themselves" in the first major episode of the Great Army's settling their conquered lands (Keynes *Vikings in England* 55). In the same year, Guthrum, Anwend, and Oscetyl went to East Anglia to take control of the kingdom with their base at Cambridge. Invasions into Wessex continued throughout the following years. Later, in 877, according to the *Chronicle*, the Viking Army in Mercia "divided the lands between themselves and Ceolwulf," suggesting that in that year, they began to settle in Mercia (Higham and Ryan 261). The most famous episode of the Great Army's invasion of England occurred in January of 878, when Guthrum, leading a "somewhat depleted force," launched the third invasion of Wessex (Higham and Ryan 56). They managed to occupy much of Wessex and were even successful at driving King Alfred, the grandson of King Ecgberht, into exile in the Somerset marches when he hid at Athelney. From there, Alfred organized a resistance and fielded an army comprised of soldiers from Somerset, Wiltshire, and Hampshire in a matter of weeks. He mounted a counter-campaign against the Viking Army, culminating at the famous Battle of Edington in Wiltshire in May 878, where he defeated Guthrum and his army. After the battle, Guthrum and "30 of his leading men" (Higham and Ryan 262) agreed to be baptized "in an extended ceremony which began at Aller near Athelney, and which was completed on the royal estate at Wedmore in Somerset" (Keynes *Vikings in England* 57). Subsequently, Guthrum and his army withdrew from Wessex to East Anglia, "where Guthrum became king" (Higham and Ryan 262) and the Vikings, once again. "settled and shared out the land" as they did in Mercia and Northumbria (Keynes *Vikings in England* 57). Later, though the exact date is not certain (perhaps in 879/80), Guthrum and Alfred struck a treaty, "drawing a boundary between their two realms up the River Thames, along the River Lea and thence up the River Ouse to Watling Street," partitioning Mercia between the

Norse and West Saxons and dividing England into West Saxon and Norse controlled territory, known as the "Danelaw" (Higham and Ryan 260-262; Downham 342-343; Keynes *Vikings in England* 54-57; Yorke 30-31).

According to the *Anglo-Saxon Chronicle,* on multiple occasions, contingents of the Great and Summer armies settled in their conquered parts of Northumbria, Mercia, and East Anglia and began to work the soil, yet the extent and nature of Norse settlement are rather opaque and difficult to track. Besides listing different settlements in Northumbria, Mercia, and East Anglia, the *Chronicle* does not provide much information, as it seems that the political status of Norse-occupied territories perplexed even Anglo-Saxon writers. A major problem persists in identifying Scandinavians post-settlement and/or invasion, especially since after the conquests of Northumbria and East Anglia, the *Chronicle* mentions the term "Dane" and refers to everyone as "Northumbrians" or "East Angles," making it difficult to ascertain to what extent the people in reference are English or Norse; they are invariably a mix with a shared geographic identity. This raises the question of *how many* Scandinavians settled England. The current consensus is that "numbers of immigrants cannot be simply deduced from their impact on the host society" (Downham 343). Instead, the strong influence that Scandinavians had on England "owes more to the duration of Viking rule and to the nature of interaction between Vikings and English" (Downham 343). There are three complementary fields crucial to tracking Norse settlements: archaeology (material evidence), genetics (blood groups and D.N.A.), and linguistics (place names and loan words) (Downham 343; Keynes, *Vikings in England* 63-68; Higham and Ryan 285-296).

The Gosforth Cross in St. Mary's Churchyard in Cumbria, England

Unlike the Anglo-Saxon settlement of Britain, there is scant material evidence of Norse settlement, though there are possible examples of artistic influence in northern England. For example, the Gosforth Cross in Cumbria is a wonderful example of syncretic North Sea Germanic and Christian imagery.[11] Unfortunately, artistic and material evidence is difficult to interpret when locating Norse settlements, though evidence exists for the emergence of an Anglo-Norse identity (Higham and Ryan 293).

Genetic evidence is still comparatively less for now since only "a small number of [D.N.A.] studies has so far been undertaken and on a limited number of sites" (Higham and Ryan 296). Blood groups and Y-chromosome-based studies of areas in the East Midlands, Wirral, and West Lancashire have discovered some genetic linkage with areas in Denmark and Norway. However, there remains a problem with genetic evidence temporally placing genetic groups. In other

---

[11] It could be argued that many secular motifs and iconography on the cross, such as armed warriors and a scene that may depict the Old Norse god Víðarr fighting the wolf Fenrir, represent an Old Norse presence in the area. Yet, these aspects "cannot be seen as the straightforward assertion of Scandinavian identity," as art styles are fluid and are not clear indicators of a specific people (styles and motifs can be shared after all!) and could also be claimed as "Anglo-Saxon motifs and forms" that point "to the continuation of native traditions and tases" (Higham and Ryan 290).

words, genetic links to Denmark could be from later Danish settlement in England and not from the Great and Summer armies (Higham and Ryan 294-96).

Linguistic evidence is just as sticky. For the most part, the current study still relies on English place-names. On the macro level, a clear division along the line of demarcation marked between Anglo-Saxon England and the Danelaw drawn up in the treaty between Alfred and Guthrum is noticeable in the spread of English place names with Norse elements in England. There are three specific categories of said place names: "Grimston Hybrids," that is, names "that combine a Scandinavian specific with the Old English generic -*tun* ("farmstead," "settlement"); names that end in -*by* from Old Norse -*býr*[12] or Old Danish -*by* ("settlement") (Keynes *Viking in England* 64); and names that end the -*thorp* ("secondary settlement"). Scandinavian place names, however, are not a clear indicator of a Norse presence. An English place name with a Norse element "need not have been named or settled by Scandinavians," as the Old Norse language had a "significant impact on Old English and many words were borrowed" (Higham and Ryan 288). For example, a fair amount of Old Norse words were borrowed into Old English, and therefore, several words in Modern English have Old Norse origins. For example, the Modern English "law," from the Old Norse *lǫg*, the verb "to egg" from *egg*, "to take" from *taka*, and even third-person pronouns "they" and "them" from *þeir, þeim,* and *þeirra* (Larrea; Pulsiano 169). Further, the problem with relying on Scandinavian place-names in England lies in issues surrounding the primary source as the first recording of said names, the *Domesday Book* of 1086. This text, composed post-Norman conquest of England, was an in-depth land survey of settlements in the Normans' recently conquered domain. Scandinavian activity was not limited to the late 9th century but continued well into the 11th century, with several English kings being Scandinavian themselves (see below). Therefore, English place-names with Norse elements need not be from the time of Great and Summer armies and their settlement(s).

Alfred the Great and the House of Wessex

The early 9th century may have seen Wessex, under King Ecgberht, rise to replace Mercia as the dominant Anglo-Saxon power. It was under Ecgberht's grandson, Alfred (later known as "the Great"), that Wessex managed to survive the 9th century's Viking invasions and secure its position within the Anglo-Saxon world into the 10th century under his descendants.

While Alfred is perhaps known to be the greatest Anglo-Saxon monarch, he did not seem destined for greatness. It was probably unlikely that he was expected to inherit the Kingdom of Wessex from his father, Æthelwulf. Alfred was the youngest of four brothers, Æthelbald, Æthelberht, Æthelred, and finally, Alfred, and each brother reigned as kings of Wessex before him. Alfred's father, Aethelwulf—though overshadowed by his father, Ecgberht—is known to have defeated an invading Viking army of around 350 ships in 851 with an army drawn from all over Wessex. He also managed to retain Wessex's hold over Kent, Sussex, Essex, and Surrey, lands his father had brought under West Saxon hegemony. Æthelwulf seems to have been a

---

[12] "-by," *wiktionary.com*, https://en.wiktionary.org/wiki/-by#English.

religious man, somewhat reserved and uninterested in ruling, as he went on pilgrimage to Rome (possibly as a part of a larger religious program "directed . . . at the Viking threat" or ecompletely unrelated) (Larrea; Pulsiano 255). in 855, "leaving the government of his kingdom to [his eldest son] Æthelbald" (Stenton 245). During this trip, he spent the summer and early autumn of 856 at the court of King Charles the Bald of the West Franks. Later, on 1 October, he married Charles's daughter, Judith, who was then 13; the marriage "should probably be regarded as nothing more than a demonstration of alliance between two kings" (Stenton 245). Upon his return journey, Æthelwulf learned that his son, Æthelbald, had seized the West Saxon throne while he was away. Æthelbald was possibly motivated to rebel by his father's marriage to Judith and the consecrating of her as queen, "an act that would have raise[d] her status above that of Æthelbald's mother" (Higham and Ryan 264). Æthelbald, therefore, may have felt threatened by the possibility of any of Judith's children holding a higher claim to the throne than him, thus leading him to rush to secure his position on the throne. Æthelbald's rebellion was resolved with father and son splitting the kingdom's rule between them, with Æthelbald over Wessex proper and Æthelwulf over Kent, Sussex, Essex, and Surrey. Later, after Æthelwulf's death in 858, Æthelbald married his father's widow, Judith, an act "contrary to Canon Law" (Higham and Ryan 264), yet nonetheless unopposed by and without "scandal among the leading churchmen of [Judith's] country" (Stenton 245). Æthelbald later died in 860 and was succeeded by his younger brother, Æthelberht, who died five years later. He, too, was succeeded by a brother, Æthelred, who reigned during the onset of the Great and Summer Armies' invasions. Together, he and Alfred fought several battles with the Vikings, winning some and losing others. However, Æthelred died in April 871, and although he left behind sons, none of them were old enough to assume immediate kingly responsibilities required in the face of the Viking incursions. Within the same year, Alfred ascended to the throne (Stenton 243-49; Higham and Ryan 264).

After defeating Guthrum and signing their treaty, which effectively divided England between Wessex and the "Danelaw", Alfred "set about ensuring that his kingdom was better protected from further Viking attacks" (Yorke *Alfred* 30). This entailed a naval building project to protect his coast and the reorganizing of the army so that "only half the force was on duty at any one time" (Yorke *Alfred* 30). The most famous project he enacted was the establishment of a system of walled fortresses and towns, called *burhs,* complete with garrisons across his kingdom. The arrangement of this building plan is recorded in a document known as the Burghal Hidage. However, this program was not complete until the reign of King Edward, Alfred's son (Yorke *Alfred* 30; Stenton 265). Alfred's reforms and building programs were, in effect, meant to widen and extend his army's maneuverability and his navy's ability to confront invading fleets (Stenton 264; Higham and Ryan 268).

Alfred,was quite aggressive and proactive in his policy toward neighboring Norse East Anglia and Northumbria, waging several wars with them. Overall, Alfred respected Guthrum's autonomy over his realm, but he was forceful in his attempts to impede East Anglian support of subsequent invading Viking armies. Alfred managed to drive off two subsequent Viking invasions, one in the autumn of 878 and another in the autumn of 892. Further, he managed to secure London through diplomacy and bring it into his sphere of influence; he married his daughter, Æthelflæd, to the ealdorman of London in 889. This ealdorman, named Æthelred, respected Alfred as his lord and subsequently presided "over the Mercian council" and lead "the Mercian armies with an authority that was never challenged" (Stenton 260). By connecting himself to a political ally and underling, Alfred allied himself with Mercia in a way that did not interfere in the autonomy of the neighboring power. Despite all diplomacy and tact, Alfred was the true leading figure in Anglo-Saxon England, and from the mid-880s, he "increasingly employed the royal style 'king of the Anglo-Saxons,'" and numismatic evidence includes titles such *rex Anglorum* (king of the English) (Higham and Ryan 266-68; Stenton 257-69; Yorke 30).

King Alfred is also significant for his intellectual contribution to the Anglo-Saxon world. Allegedly, by the time he had come into his throne in 871, the state of education, learning, and Latinity had declined so much that "no one south of the Thames could understand the liturgy or translate Latin into English" (Higham and Ryan 251). Alfred himself could not read Latin, as much of his life had been devoted to combating the Norse in England, so when things began to settle after years of fighting between Wessex and its Norse-lead neighbors in addition to invading Viking fleets, Alfred began a program meant to reform and reinvigorate learning and literacy within his domains. To do this, he invited various learned men, such as Fulco, archbishop of Reims, and Grimbald, the monk from the monastery of St. Bertin at St. Omer, to his court to spearhead the project. Complimentary to this program, Alfred also made several literary contributions to the revival of Anglo-Saxon learning. This was possible after Alfred learned Latin between 887 and 893 by "listening to one or other of the scholars whom he had called to his court" (Stenton 272). Alfred's works were translations of Gregory the Great's *Pastoral Care* (*Cura Pastoralis*), Orosius's *Seven Books of History Against the Pagans* (*Historiae Adversus Paganos*), the Venerable Bede's *Ecclesiastical History* (*Historia Ecclesiastica*), Boethius's *Consolation of Philosophy* (*De Consolatione Philosophiae*), St. Augustine of Hippo's *Soliloquies*, and the first 50 psalms into Old English, his native language. Alfred's rendition of Orosius's *Histories* provides an interesting treasure trove of information, as he expanded the original text "into what became almost a new book" to include primary source information on the "countries and peoples of northern and central Europe" (Stenton 273). Further, the position of the translation of Bede in the corpus of Alfred's work is doubted since there are many linguistic qualities in the earliest form of the text that would suggest a different place of composition by someone who spoke the Anglian dialect of Old English. Whatever the case, Alfred's translations combined with his own prefaces provide a unique look into the mind of an Anglo-Saxon king and convey someone who was deeply religious and concerned for his kingdom's well-being. Alfred also composed "new laws" for his domains that were rather conservative and traditional, as they were comprised of—and were a direct continuation of—the laws of Ine of Wessex, Offa of Mercia, and Æthelberht of Kent. Alfred the Great, therefore, remains a gigantic historical figure who set a precedent for successive models of Christian kingship far removed from the tribal and Pagan kingship of early Anglo-Saxon England (Higham and Ryan 251, 262-70; Stenton 269-276).

King Alfred the Great of Wessex died on 26 October 899; he was succeeded by Edward, his eldest son, "known since the end of the eleventh century as 'Edward the Elder'" (Stenton 269-276). However, Edward's succession was neither smooth nor uncontested. In his cousin, Æthelwold (c. 868-903), son of King Æthelred (d. 871), brother of Alfred, "Edward faced a serious rival for the throne" who was able to "command considerable loyalty and support" in the kingdom (Stenton 296). Æthelwold pressed his claim to the throne through arms, seizing the residences of Wimborne and Christchurch in Dorset upon Alfred's death. Edward matched his cousin with an army of his own. Later, Æthelwold traveled to Northumbria, where the Danish Army accepted him as their king, possibly in the hope of establishing a puppet ruler in Wessex, like they had done with Ceolwulf in Mercia. Next, in 901, Æthelwold "landed with a fleet in Essex" and in 903, convinced the Danes of East Anglia to "break peace with Edward." Fighting in Mercia and Wessex broke out, and Edward, in turn, "ravaged parts of Cambridgeshire" (Stenton 297). Neither side engaged the other in open battle, however. The conflict reached its climax when, during Edward's withdrawal from East Anglia, the Kentish contingent of his army "lingered behind" and was attacked by Æthelwold's forces (Keynes *England, c. 900-1016* 461). Despite a Danish victory, this battle ("of Holme") resulted in heavy casualties on both sides. The losses on Æthelwold's side were comprised of Eorhic (possibly the king of East Anglia), a certain Brihtsige, "probably a scion of one of the ruling dynasties of Mercia," and Æthelwold himself (Keynes *England, c. 900-1016* 461; Higham and Ryan 297). Although the *Anglo-Saxon Chronicle* claims that Æthelwold's push for the throne was an act of rebellion against his cousin and king, Edward's claim to the throne in 899 was tenuous and not yet secured (he was not crowned until June 8, 900, a ceremony which greatly solidified his legitimacy), and Æthelwold potentially had just as good a claim to the throne, judging by the extent of his support among the nobility in Wessex. Therefore, Æthelwold's play for the West Saxon throne can be seen as a bid against a rival, uncrowned claimant rather than a rebellion against a rightful monarch (Higham and Ryan 296-297; Keynes *England, c. 900-1016* 459-61).

According to contemporary charters, Edward seems to have inherited the Alfredian polity of the king of the Angles and the Saxons, throwing the exact nature of just *what* exactly Edward inherited into question. Regardless, Edward seems to have held authority over the joint West Saxon and Mercian territories that Alfred more-or-less ruled. A considerable amount of autonomy and authority was wielded by Edward's brother-in-law Æthelred, the aforementioned ealdorman of London and Mercia, and sister, Æthelflæd. There is a level of propaganda-esque discrepancy between the native annals of Wessex and Mercia; the "one-sided views of the chroniclers were the natural product of their partisan interest" and should, therefore, be seen as "complementary accounts" of a larger whole (Keynes *England, c. 900-1016* 264). The *Mercian Register* and the *Annals of Æthelflæd* depict Edward's sister as a successful and headstrong ruler of Mercia, able to resist Vikings and Welsh alike after her husband Æthelred's death in 911. However, the *Chronicle* treats Edward as a sole and indisputable ruler, and numismatic evidence in Mercia attests to Edward as king, not Æthelred and Æthelflæd (Higham and Ryan 297-298; Keynes *England, c. 900-1016* 463-464).

Edward and his sister shared a mutually benefactive relationship, and both greatly contributed to the expansion of Wessex into previously Danish controlled territory in the 10th century. Throughout his reign, Edward conducted campaigns against East Anglia, the Danish controlled Mercia, and Northumbria. Edward and Æthelflæd were particularly successful in penetrating and controlling parts of central England from the Wirral to the Thames estuary, through the strategic construction of *burhs*, which created zones of influence, and through encouraging "thegns to purchase lands in Viking-controlled territories" such as Bedfordshire and Derbyshire (Higham and Ryan 299). Later, with Æthelflæd's death in 918, according to the *Mercian Register*, "all the Danish armies south of the Humber, with the exception of those based at Nottingham and perhaps Lincoln, had submitted either to Edward or Æthelflæd" (Keynes *England, c. 900-1016* 465). Later, Essex, East Anglia, Northampton, Bedford, Huntingdon, and Cambridge submitted to Edward. Further, Æthelflæd had gained the submission of Derby, Leicester, and York. After his sister's death in 918, Edward is said to have assumed direct control of all English Mercia's territories. The *Chronicle* claims that in 920, Scotland, Northumbria ("both [the] English and Danish"), and the Welsh kingdom of Strathclyde submitted to Edward. This event is probably misrepresented by the *Chronicle,* and instead, the participants "may have seen it more as the negotiation of a peace treaty" (Higham and Ryan 301). Edward, therefore, may have held only nominal authority over Northumbria, a land which was still politically fractured. The incorporation of Northumbria into the kingdom of the House of Wessex would be the work of another king, Edward's son and successor, Æthelstan (Higham and Ryan 298-301; Keynes *England, c. 900-1016* 465-66; Miller 167).

Æthelstan, First King of England?

Edward died in June 924, and his domains were seemingly split between his sons Æthelstan—recognized as king by the Mercians—and Ælfweard—recognized as king by the West Saxons. It is "far from clear" why this split occurred, or if it was Edward's wish that his domains be divided among his songs (Keynes *England, c. 900-1016* 467). The split may be related to competing partisan interests from Mercia and Wessex, as Æthelstan possibly struggled to woo the West Saxon nobility and clergy—with their power centered at the court in Winchester—a struggle which was just as possibly related to his birth and upbringing. Æthelstan was the son of King Edward and a "woman considered to be of low birth," and he was raised at the court of his uncle and aunt, Æthelred and Æthelflæd, the Lord and Lady of Mercia (Keynes *England, c. 900-1016* 467). Ælfweard was, however, a legitimate son of Edward's, and it should not be disregarded that this possibly contributed to an assumed tension between the half-brothers and their respective parties. Æthelstan's identity, therefore, was that of a partial outsider—undoubtedly a part of the West Saxon dynasty, but isolated "from the West Saxon establishment at Winchester" (in which he experienced political resistance among the clergy) with his background in the Mercian political sphere (Keynes *England, c. 900-1016* 468). Ælfweard soon died, and Æthelstan inherited his half of the Alfredian kingdom of the Anglo-Saxons. He was crowned at Kingston-upon-Thames (a location conspicuously on the border between Wessex and Mercia) on

4 September 925 (Keynes *England, c. 900-1016* 466-468; Higham and Ryan 301; Miller *Æthelstan* 17-18).

Æthelstan inherited the kingdom of the Angles and the Saxons from his father, Edward, as he had from his father, Alfred. After Ælfweard's death, Æthelstan consolidated his land and went on to conquer Northumbria "with apparent ease" (Higham and Ryan 302). First, he formed an alliance with King Sihtric of Northumbria, located in York, through marriage to the Norse king in 926. This alliance was short-lived, however, as Sihtric died in 927. Afterward, according to the "D" version of the *Chronicle*, Æthelstand inherited his new brother-in-laws' lands, bringing Northumbria under his control. It is ambiguous whether Æthelstan merely seized the opportunity of a "political vacuum" to claim Northumbria or succeeded Sihtric, according to a "prior agreement" of succession (Keynes *England, c. 900-1016* 468). The "E" version of the *Chronicle* records also that "in the same year Æthelstan 'drove out King Guthfrith,'" a Viking king active in both Britain and Ireland (Higham and Ryan 302). The *Chronicle* also reports that Æthelstan's northerly ambitions did not stop at Northumbria. Allegedly, on 12 July 927, at "a place called Eamont" he "'brought under his rule all the kings who were in this island:'" the kings of the Britons of Strathclyde, the Welsh, and Scots (Keynes *England, c. 900-1016* 469; Miller *Æthelstan* 18). Æthelstan's charters thenceforth call him *rex Anglorum* (king of the English) and *rex totius Britannia* (king of the whole of Britain), the latter appearing on his coins, as well; later, a certain poem celebrating "the events of 927 alludes to *ista perfecta Saxonica* ('this England now made whole')" (Keynes *England, c. 900-1016* 469). Æthelstan's alleged peace with the Scots, Britons, and Norse, who had a claim to and interest in Northumbria, was short-lived. In 934, he invaded Scotland, "attacking as far north as Kincardine and by the sea Caithness," for unknown reasons (Higham and Ryan 303). Just three years later, in 937, King Constantine I of Scotland, King Owain of Strathclyde, and King Olaf Guthfrithsson of Dublin invaded Æthelstan's kingdom in a bid to reclaim the Viking kingdom of York. Æthelstan, and his brother Edmund, with an army comprised of West Saxons and Mercians, defeated the invading army at the Battle of *Brunanburh* (location unknown), an event recorded in an Old English poem redacted in the *Chronicle,* as well as the Icelandic *Egil's Saga* (in Old Norse *Egils saga skallagrímssonar*). Although the battle seems a decisive end to the conflict in posterity, Æthelstan's hold on Northumbria was far from firm or complete, as the area still remained politically fractured and dominated by various political and religious factions and authorities, such as the archbishop of York. Æthelstan was, therefore, careful to appease the various factions, cultivating, for example, "the support of the community of St. Cuthbert, visiting the saint's shrine" (Higham and Ryan 303). Northumbria would remain throughout Æthelstan and his successor's reigns a slippery political territory, changing hands several times (Higham and Ryan 303).

Æthelstan's reign stands in sharp contrast to that of his father in terms of charters, which provide a richer and deeper look into his reign than the "Edwardian gap"; there are simply scan charters from Edward's reign (Keynes *England, c. 900-1016* 469). Æthelstan was instrumental in the development of law in the kingdom of the Angles and the Saxons, and seven law codes from his reign survive to this day. Further, like the court of his grandfather, Æthelstan's court was the destination of a plethora of foreigners. He fostered Alan of Britanny and Hakon, the son of King Harald of Norway, and formed marriage alliances with the royal families of Francia and Germany. Scholars and travelers from Italy, Germany, Ireland, Francia, Brittany, and Iceland, specifically the famous warrior-poet Egill Skallagrímsson, were hosted at his court. Although traditionally, Æthelstan is overshadowed by the likes of Alfred, it is with him that the notion of the kingdom of England took root. Although his grasp on a unified territory reflective of the later medieval kingdom of England was tenuous, Æthelstan set the ball rolling toward the formation of the English kingdom for his descendants. Yet, "the crucial developments took place in the twenty years which followed King Æthelstan's death" (Keynes *England, c. 900-1016* 471). He died on 27 October 939 and was subsequently buried at Malmesbury (Keynes *England, c. 900-1016* 469-71; Higham and Ryan 303; Miller *Æthelstan* 18).

Æthelred was succeeded by his brother, Edmund, in 939, who lost Northumbria to Olaf Guthfrithssom, who returned from Ireland "and was accepted as king" (Higham and Ryan 303). Edmund managed to reconquer Northumbria and throw out its Norse rulers, but the region proved difficult to retain through regnal succession. In other words, the next king often had to retake what the previous king had conquered. This was the case with Edmund's successor Eadred (r. 946-55), Æthelstan and Edmund's brother. Further, the Northumbrians during the reigns of Alfred's descendants were able to exercise considerable autonomy and authority, reestablishing their independence under Norse rulers such as Olaf Sihtricsson, Olaf Guthrithsson, and exiled King Eirik Bloodaxe of Norway, whom the Northumbrians accepted as king in York 947 (*Keynes England, c. 900-1016* 473). This pattern persisted during Eadred's reign, with the Northumbrians submitting to Eadred (946), then Eirik Bloodaxe (947), then Eadred again (948), then Olaf Sihtricsson (950/1), then Eirik again (952), and then Eadred for the last time (954). It is to Eadred that the unification of England, with Northumbria finally coming into the House of Wessex's fold for good, was completed "nearly three decades after the submission to Æthelstan in 927" (Keynes *Eadred* 154). However, England was far from being politically united. In the 950s, it was divided between Edmund's son, Eadwig, "ruling south of the Thames," and "his older brother, Edgar, reigning in Mercia and the north" (Higham and Ryan 304). The division between north and south and the division between rulers would persist into Danish and Anglo-Danish rule of England in 1016 and again in the 1030s. Regardless, upon Eadwig's death, Edgar inherited the whole kingdom: "The kingdom of England as it stood at the end of Edgar's reign has to be seen, then, as the product of a series of contingent events, as created by chance and compromise far more than by any overall royal design or strategy." (Higham and Ryan 305)

The kind of Anglo-Saxon England in which Alfred and his descendants lived and ruled proved to be greatly changed. During the dominance of the House of Wessex, Anglo-Saxon England experienced sharp changes in nobility, law, and church. The 10th century in England "saw the emergence of a number of particularly powerful noble families," who held a number of offices and dominated "royal administration and government" (Higham and Ryan 310). Further, Alfred's legal legacy was carried on by his descendants, notably Æthelstan, during whose reign several law-codes bearing his name were drafted, such as *II Æthelstan*, which "records pronouncements made at a royal council at Greatly [Hampshire]," covering issues such as justice, minting of coins, and the "purchasing of livestock" (Higham and Ryan 306). What is important concerning legal changes in 10th century England is that the "promulgation of law became a form of communication between the king, his advisor, and subjects" (Higham and Ryan 306). Lastly, the 10th century was also witness to what is called the Benedictine Reforms, which reached "their peak in the reign of Edgar" (Higham and Ryan 312). These reforms resulted in an increase in monasticism and in monastic communities in England adhering to the Rule of St. Benedict of Nursia, the founder of the Benedictine order and after whom the reforms are named. Specifically, the aim of the reforms was to replace religious centers that were dominated by "communities of clerks—that is, members of the clerical orders"—with monastic communities (Higham and Ryan 312). The issue with clerical orders was their domination by laymen, "who appropriated their estates and sapped their wealth" (Higham and Ryan 312). The 10th century in England was an age of drastic change in which England began to resemble a continental Christian kingdom.

Late Anglo-Saxon England

When King Edgar died on July 8, 975, his realm was thrown into conflict among the different factions. Edgar was succeeded by his son Edward, whom Byrhtferth of Ramsey, the author of the *Life of St. Oswald*, characterized as one who "struck fear and terror into everyone and hounded them not only with tongue-lashing but even with cruel beatings" (Higham and Ryan 338). Edward was not long for this world, however, as he was murdered and succeeded by his half-brother Æthelred (later known as the "Unready"), who would become one of the most controversial Anglo-Saxon kings (Higham and Ryan 336-338).

A coin bearing King Æthelred's image minted as the Cissbury mint

The narrative of Æthelred's reign is dominated by the renewal of Viking raids in England, which resumed in the 980s and had their culmination in King Svein Forkbeard of Denmark's conquest of England and the exiling of Æthelred to Normandy in 1013-14. The earlier phases of raiding escalated in 991 at the famous Battle of Maldon in Essex, where the Ealdorman

Bryhtnoth repelled a Viking Army of 90 ships led by Olaf Tryggvason (later king of Norway in 995) and possibly King Svein of Denmark. The battle cost Bryhtnoth his life, but his "doomed bravery" was praised in the Old English poem, *The Battle of Maldon* (Higham and Ryan 343). Æthelred's reign was plagued by these Viking raids, and the king often resorted to payments of tribute, which have "contributed considerably to Æthelred's poor reputation" (Higham and Ryan 346). Æthelred did make noticeable attempts to strengthen England's defenses against Denmark and Norway's prolonged offensive. Some of his methods were quite cruel and extreme, such as the infamous St. Brice's Day Massacre on 13 November 1002, where Æthelred reportedly "ordered that 'all Danish men who were in England' were to be slain" (Higham and Ryan 347). This decree was, by no means, an act on par with policies of genocide in the modern era, as it did not target Scandinavian descendants living in England who were fully integrated into the Anglo-Saxon world. Rather, the grim massacre was a direct targeting of recent Danish settlers and Vikings active in England at the time. It was, therefore, another example of how the apparatus of violence was employed by kings in the ruling of the Anglo-Saxon state. Yet, the undeniable fact is that Æthelred eventually failed, and his reign ended in disaster: the conquest of his realm. This, therefore, has contributed heavily to his bad reputation as a poor ruler, reinforced by his cognomen the "Unready" (a later 12th-century invention).[13] It should be considered that Æthelred's bad reputation is, in part, due to the versions of the *Chronicle* recounting the narrative of his reign. The C, D, and E versions of the *Chronicle* are not contemporary to Æthelred's reign and were probably composed during the reign of Cnut (1016-35), "looking back on Æthelred's reign with the full knowledge that it would end in disaster, defeat, and conquest" (Higham and Ryan 340). Despite how his reign concluded, he should be credited with lasting the Viking onslaught as long as he did (Higham and Ryan 339-351; Keynes *England, 900-1016* 483-484; Miller *Æthelred the Unready* 16-17).

In 1009, a Viking army led by Thorkell the Tall "ravaged southern England" and exacted tribute in 1012. In 1013, this invasion was followed by King Svein Forkbeard of Denmark's invasion of England, ending in Æthelred's exile and Svein on the English throne. King Svein's reign was short-lived, as he died on 3 February 1014, and he was succeeded by his son, Cnut, (also spelled Knut and Canute). There was a scuffle for the English throne, with Æthelred returning from exile and the thegns in the kingdom electing their own claimant. All this was snuffed out when Cnut returned to England with an army in 1015. Æthelred died in April 1016, and on 18 October 1016, England was split between Edmund Ironside (Æthelred's son) and Cnut, who became king of Mercia. Edmund later died in November 1016, leaving England open to Cnut. Starting in 1017, he consolidated his position as king of England, dividing England into four regions: Wessex, East Anglia, Mercia, and Northumbria. He kept Wessex for himself and married Æthelred's second wife, Emma, granting her a title to secure her position and undermine Edward and Alfred's descendants. Cnut's reign is remarkable in how, at its height, he controlled territories all over the North Sea and Northern Europe: England, Denmark, Norway, and parts of

---

[13] Æthelred means 'noble counsel' and the nickname 'Unræd,' which means 'no counsel' or 'ill-counselled,' is a pun or play on his name (Higham and Ryan 335).

southern Sweden. He was able to reorganize and restructure England's government and society, fostering in an era of Anglo-Danish culture and drafting law codes. His reign should be studied in its own right beyond this *very* brief and scant summary of his rule. He died at Shaftesbury in Dorset on November 12, 1035 and was succeeded by his sons, Harthacnut and Harold Harefoot, who split the rule of England between them with the former getting the south and the latter the north. Harthacnut was, however, absent from the treaty at Oxford that decided this, as he was in Denmark securing his position as king. He did not return for some time, with Harold becoming the *de facto* ruler of England. However, Harthacnut returned to England in 1040 upon his brother's death to claim the English throne. During the period of the later 10th and early 11th century, despite the violence and political upheaval caused by Danish and Anglo-Saxon struggles for the throne, England experienced a "period in which many prospered" and it "remained a wealthy kingdom" to be desired by the later claimants of the massively famous struggle that was 1066 (Higham and Ryan 373, 349-52, 358-65; Keynes *Cnut* 111-112).

Conclusion

It is difficult to do justice to the immense stretch of Anglo-Saxon history. It is a period of history foundational to the story of England. It is ultimately the story of migration and change, with people going back and forth across the North Sea and setting up polities of their own to compete for larger swathes of land. It was also a period of literature and not a dark age, as some might say. The Anglo-Saxons gave the world Bede and *Beowulf*, riddles and art, and a veritable hoard of literature that can still be enjoyed and studied today. Interest in the Anglo-Saxons has been on the rise ever since the 18th century, with famous figures from Thomas Jefferson to J. R. R. Tolkien taking a personal or academic interest in them. Today, demands for stories from this time period never seem to wane as people flock to shows like *The Last Kingdom* and games like *Assassin's Creed: Valhalla*. The authors hope that they have instilled in the readers some interest of their own and recommend the reader consult further and more extensive sources on the period, such as those from this article's bibliography.

Online Resources

Other books about medieval history by Charles River Editors

Other books about English history by Charles River Editors

Other books about the Anarchy on Amazon

Further Reading

Bill, Jan. "Ships and Seamanship." *The Oxford Illustrated History of the Vikings*. Edited by Peter Sawyer. New York: Oxford University Press, 1999. pp. 182-201.
Brink, Stefan. "Who Where the Vikings." *The Viking World*. Edited by Stefan Brink and Neil

Price. New York: Routledge, 2012. pp. 4-7.

Coupland, Simon. "Vikings in Francia and Anglo-Saxon England to 911." *New Cambridge Medieval History* vol. 2. Edited by Paul Fouracre. Cambridge University Press, 2008. pp. 190-201.

Downham, Clare. "Vikings in England." *The Viking World.* Edited by Stefan Brink and Neil Price. New York: Routledge, 2012. pp. 341-349.

Dudo of St. Quentin. *History of the Normans.* Translated by E. Christiansen. Woodbridge, Suffolk: Boydell, 1998. pp. 15-17.

Dumville, David and Simon Keynes general eds. *The Anglo-Saxon Chronicle: A Collaborative Edition.* Translated by A.A. Somerville. Cambridge: D.S. Brewer, 2004. pp.41-46.

English Historical Documents c. 500-1041. Edited by D. Whitelock. London: Eyre & Spottiswoode, 1955. pp. 775-77.

Garrison, Mary. "Alcuin of York." *The Wiley Blackwell Encyclopedia of Anglo-Saxon England 2nd ed.* Edited by Michael Lapidge, John Blair, Simon Keynes, and Donald Scragg. Chichester, West Sussex: Blackwell, 2014. pp. 26-27.

Haywood, John. *Encyclopedia of the Viking Age.* New York: Thames and Hudson, 2000.

Higham, Nicholas J. and Martin J. Ryan. *The Anglo-Saxon World.* Yale University Press, 2013.

Keynes, Simon. "Coenwulf." *The Wiley Blackwell Encyclopedia of Anglo-Saxon England 2nd ed.* Edited by Michael Lapidge, John Blair, Simon Keynes, and Donald Scragg. Chichester, West Sussex: Blackwell, 2014. pp. 114-15.

Keynes, Simon. "Cnut." *The Wiley Blackwell Encyclopedia of Anglo-Saxon England 2nd ed.* Edited by Michael Lapidge, John Blair, Simon Keynes, and Donald Scragg. Chichester, West Sussex: Blackwell, 2014. pp. 111-12.

Keynes, Simon. "Eadred." *The Wiley Blackwell Encyclopedia of Anglo-Saxon England 2nd ed.* Edited by Michael Lapidge, John Blair, Simon Keynes, and Donald Scragg. Chichester, West Sussex: Blackwell, 2014. pp. 154-55.

Keynes, Simon. "England, 700-900." *New Cambridge Medieval History* vol. 2. Edited by Paul Fouracre. Cambridge University Press, 2008. pp. 18-42.

Keynes, Simon. "England, c. 900-1016." *New Cambridge Medieval History* vol. 2. Edited by Paul Fouracre. Cambridge University Press, 2008. pp. 456-484.

Keynes, Simon. "The Vikings in England." *The Oxford Illustrated History of the Vikings.* Edited by Peter Sawyer. New York: Oxford University Press, 1999. pp. 48-82.

Larrea, Beñat Elortza. "Medieval Scandinavia: Assemblies, Law-giving, and Language." *medievalist.net.* https://www.medievalists.net/2020/07/assemblies-law-giving-language/. accessed 14 August 2020.

Lönnroth, Lars. "The Vikings in History and Legend." *The Oxford Illustrated History of the Vikings.* Edited by Peter Sawyer. New York: Oxford University Press, 1999. pp. 225-249.

Miller, Sean. "Æthelred the Unready." *The Wiley Blackwell Encyclopedia of Anglo-Saxon England 2ⁿᵈ ed.* Edited by Michael Lapidge, John Blair, Simon Keynes, and Donald Scragg. Chichester, West Sussex: Blackwell, 2014. pp. 16-17.

Miller, Sean. "Æthelstan." *The Wiley Blackwell Encyclopedia of Anglo-Saxon England 2ⁿᵈ ed.* Edited by Michael Lapidge, John Blair, Simon Keynes, and Donald Scragg. Chichester, West Sussex: Blackwell, 2014. pp. 17-18.

Miller, Sean. "Edward the Elder." *The Wiley Blackwell Encyclopedia of Anglo-Saxon England 2ⁿᵈ ed.* Edited by Michael Lapidge, John Blair, Simon Keynes, and Donald Scragg. Chichester, West Sussex: Blackwell, 2014. p. 167.

Mostert Marco. "Edmund, St, King of East Anglia." *The Wiley Blackwell Encyclopedia of Anglo-Saxon England 2ⁿᵈ ed.*, eds. Michael Lapidge, John Blair, Simon Keynes, and Donald Scragg, Blackwell, 2014.

Pulsiano, Phillip. "England, Norse in." *Medieval Scandinavia: An Encyclopedia.* Edited by Phillip Pulsiano. New York: Garland Publishing, 1993. pp. 166-170.

Sawyer, Peter. "The Age of the Vikings and Before." *The Oxford Illustrated History of the Vikings.* Edited by Peter Sawyer. New York: Oxford University Press, 1999. pp. 1-18.

Somerville, A.A trans. *A Second Anglo-Saxon Reader: Archaic and Dialectal.* Edited by Henry Sweet. Revised by T.F. Hoad. Oxford: Clarendon Press, 1978.

Stafford, Pauline. "Reeve." *The Wiley Blackwell Encyclopedia of Anglo-Saxon England 2ⁿᵈ ed.* Edited by Michael Lapidge, John Blair, Simon Keynes, and Donald Scragg. Chichester, West Sussex: Blackwell, 2014. pp. 397-98.

Stenton, F. M. *Anglo-Saxon England 3ʳᵈ ed.* New York: Oxford University Press, 2004.

The Viking Age: A Reader 2ⁿᵈ ed. Edited by Angus A. Somerville and R. Andrew McDonald. Toronto: University of Toronto Press, 2014.

Williams, Gareth. "Raiding and Warfare." *The Viking World.* Edited by Stefan Brink and Neil Price. New York: Routledge, 2012. pp. 193-204.

Yorke, B. A. E. "Alfred, King of Wessex." *The Wiley Blackwell Encyclopedia of Anglo-Saxon England 2ⁿᵈ ed.* Edited by Michael Lapidge, John Blair, Simon Keynes, and Donald Scragg. Chichester, West Sussex: Blackwell, 2014. pp. 29-31.

Yorke, B. A. E., "Ecgberht, king of Wessex." *The Wiley Blackwell Encyclopedia of Anglo-Saxon England 2ⁿᵈ ed.* Edited by Michael Lapidge, John Blair, Simon Keynes, and Donald Scragg. Chichester, West Sussex: Blackwell, 2014. p. 162

Free Books by Charles River Editors

We have brand new titles available for free most days of the week. To see which of our titles are currently free, click on this link.

Discounted Books by Charles River Editors

We have titles at a discount price of just 99 cents everyday. To see which of our titles are currently 99 cents, click on this link.

Printed in Great Britain
by Amazon